LIFE *in the* FLOCK *of* GEASCHELS

Pure Faith

Christine Geaschel

WESTBOW
P R E S S®
A DIVISION OF THOMAS NELSON
& ZONDERVAN

WestBow Press books may be ordered through booksellers or by contacting:

WestBow Press
A Division of Thomas Nelson & Zondervan
1663 Liberty Drive
Bloomington, IN 47403
www.westbowpress.com
844-714-3454

Interior Image Credit: Photography Christine Geaschel and Britta Fuzak

ISBN: 978-1-6642-4434-4 (sc)
ISBN: 978-1-6642-4436-8 (hc)
ISBN: 978-1-6642-4435-1 (e)

Library of Congress Control Number: 2021918310

Print information available on the last page.

WestBow Press rev. date: 10/26/2021

This book is dedicated to our Lord and Savior, Jesus Christ, and to our daughter, Karina Faith (Pure Faith).

Introduction

This is the story of our sweet little miracle baby. We believe that life begins at conception, so her story starts even before she was born. Even before her conception and before time began, her life story was planned out by our God. Her written story is not complete without God's hand weaving its way through it, as He is the Creator and the Sustainer of her life. Please sit back, relax, and enjoy the story of *Life in the Flock of Geaschels: Pure Faith.*

1

"I WON'T BE ABLE TO deliver your baby at home. You will have to go see a doctor." Those words that were spoken by the midwife would drastically change our summer and impact all of our lives. As I was lying on the midwife's exam table, with my husband holding my hand, and our children playing quietly in another room, I felt like I was in a nightmare, one from which I couldn't awaken.

The precious baby that I was carrying was our eighth. This was supposed to be our second home birth. We were looking forward to the peaceful, drug-free atmosphere that we had experienced with this baby's sister just fifteen months earlier, but then my current pregnancy had been different from the beginning.

I had only wanted an ultrasound so that I might have peace of mind in our decision to take the kids on a trip to Virginia. It was the four hundredth anniversary of the founding of Jamestown, and we planned for the whole family to be a part of that exciting celebration. Our children's names were engraved on a memorial plaque that was going to be unveiled during the celebration, and we hoped to be a part of that momentous occasion. During our planned stay in Virginia, my husband, Bill, was also planning to take part in a reenactment of the second Virginia Convention, with about a dozen other men and boys.

I had already started packing and filling the living room with bins of nonperishable food and small suitcases of clothing because I knew that packing for nine people while being pregnant was going to take me a few weeks. We would be taking most of our food with us because eating out was so costly and time consuming with a large family.

Our planned trip was only a couple of weeks away, and our baby was due shortly after we returned home. As I look back, I realize that I had been having thoughts for a while that something was not right. I just had not been sure what it was. I was not worried about going into labor while we were away because all our other seven children had been born late. I had never had any contractions prior to my due dates. There was no reason to believe that I would go into labor early this time, but I wanted to know where the placenta was located.

I also had concerns about the baby's position. I thought that if I was due soon, the baby should have descended farther into place than I felt that she was. I mostly wanted to know where everything was positioned before embarking on our cross-country journey. I already had contact info for midwives who lived in the states that we would be traveling through, in case I did go into labor while we were away, but it didn't ease my gut feelings of question and concern.

Earlier in the week at my bimonthly checkup when I told the midwife I wanted an ultrasound, she questioned me. "Why do you want an ultrasound?" I told her of my concerns, especially in regard to traveling so far, and she helped me find another midwife nearby, who gave inexpensive ultrasounds for home-birth moms.

We went for the ultrasound. When we first arrived, we had all our children with us in the room. I was so excited to show them their new sibling, who we expected would join us four weeks later. This was the first one that many of them had seen. As we watched the screen, we excitedly saw our precious baby. The technician pointed out the legs, the arms, and the spine. Everything seemed to look perfect.

Then at one point, Bill and the technician became quiet. We realized that when we were looking at the baby's face, something was wrong. The eyes were easily located, and we saw the nose, but below the nose going all the way to the chest, there was a dark area. The technician scanned the face a few more times and then stepped out of the room. We sent our seven children out of the room to play.

I do not remember what happened during those next few seconds or was it minutes or hours? But during that time, the technician called our midwife and told her what she had found. The technician then returned to my bedside holding a cordless phone, and my midwife talked to me on the phone and gave me the news. She told me that there was something seriously wrong with the baby and that we needed to go to a physician who would take us through the rest of the pregnancy and perform a hospital delivery. She said that the technician felt there was some kind of mass or teratoma on or in the baby's mouth.

We were also informed that the baby had some fluid around the heart and that the baby was not as far along as it should be. There was a difference of about five weeks. *Five weeks?* I wondered how the baby could be five weeks smaller than it should be. My midwife reluctantly told us that there was no chance of a home birth and that I might even have to have a C-section. Now the scheduled trip to Virginia was also questionable.

I was in shock. I realized that the next few weeks would be crucial to the future of this precious little one. At that stage in my life, I started wanting things to be more natural and with less doctor intervention, so this was very hard to swallow. *A C-section?* I thought. I had never even had an epidural because I did not want drugs, or needles, or anything more than what was necessary.

A C-section? A hospital? What about our quiet natural living room delivery with the family all around me, which we are preparing for? I wondered. Everything seemed to be so overwhelming. I felt as if my head was spinning.

During that life-changing phone call, the children had been playing quietly in another room, and they knew of no problems. They became worried when they returned to the room and both Mommy and Daddy were crying. It was hard to know what to say and how to explain the news to them. They had been so excited to see our new baby on the ultrasound. We had to figure out how to tell them that there was something very wrong with our precious baby and that Mommy would have to go to the hospital for more tests.

We also did not want to scare them, but to let them know that we trusted God in whatever happened with this precious baby in the upcoming weeks and months. As we explained what we could, some of our kids understood, but the youngest ones did not have a clue what was going on. They only understood that we needed prayer. The hardest news for them was that we might not be going on our trip to Virginia.

On the way home from our ultrasound, we all prayed together. I called both sets of our parents to inform them of our urgent need for prayer. As soon as we arrived home, I immediately went to my computer and sent out emails asking for prayer... to family members, church friends, and anyone else who I knew would pray for us. The emails that I first wrote ended up eventually being added onto a CarePages website, which I set up. It was a long-term way to efficiently update everyone, share our prayer requests, and report answered prayers along the way.

Excerpt from CarePages

June 2, 2007

Dear family and friends, we could use your prayers for our little baby.

I went in for an ultrasound today because things didn't seem right. We found out that the baby has a large growth on its cheek and fluid surrounding its heart. The baby measures at thirty-one weeks, when I am actually thirty-six weeks.

Please be in prayer with us for the following:

- *That the growth would miraculously disappear or that we would be able to have it taken care of with no complications once the baby is born*
- *That the growth will not interfere with nursing (I have had enough problems with that in the past)*
- *That my dates are off, and the baby isn't as small as we think it is*
- *That the fluid surrounding its heart wouldn't be a problem or that the fluid would disappear on its own*
- *That I would have peace about the hospital birth and the possible C-section*
- *That we would accept the possibility that we might not go on our planned trip to Virginia*

In Christ,
Christie for the Geaschel family

During this time, Psalm 139 became very important to me in praying for our baby. I read that chapter often and thanked God that even though I did not know what was going on, He did. This baby was in His hands.

Just a few days later, we had an appointment with a doctor who would take me this late in the pregnancy and not be upset by our planned home birth. I was so relieved that they accepted me and did not seem to discriminate against me and the fact that I had planned to have the baby at home. The technician who had done our first ultrasound worked for this physician too. She did another ultrasound for us with a more high-tech machine.

We were so excited to go to the first doctor's appointment. We anticipated that the many questions that we had would be answered. To our surprise, again the baby had a dark area from its nose to its neck.

I thought, *What is this? Is it inside or coming out of the mouth? Is there a mouth?* I still had lots of questions but no real answers. One question was answered regarding the baby's gender. The baby was a girl, and we named her Karina Faith. We knew she would need many prayers, and we chose a name that means *pure faith*. We knew that only God could help her, heal her, and sustain her, and we would depend on Him for her little life.

We also found out that the fluid around her heart was gone and that her heart seemed perfectly normal. This was the first of many answered prayers. On the way home from that appointment, we found ourselves driving behind a car with a license plate that read, "Karina." The car's plate solidified our chosen name for our precious baby.

At the first appointment, the doctor told us that it would not be a good idea to go to Virginia before the baby's birth. The children were sad, but they also understood the reason that we couldn't go. After a few days, Bill and I decided that we should be able to go camping closer to home for the weekend, especially since I already had food and clothes packed for all of us.

We went to a nearby state park with some dear friends. We had a wonderful time- fishing, hiking, cooking out, and playing. After we got home from our special weekend, we were praying as a family. When it was Elaina's (age four) turn, she said, "Dear God, thank you that we got to go to Virginia." I realized that camping close to home wasn't too bad of a decision, at least for the youngest three children.

After a couple of visits to the doctor, he realized that he would not be able to perform the delivery. He did not have enough information from the ultrasound images or any experience with someone in Karina's condition. He sent me to the maternal-fetal clinic at another hospital in our town. I remember thinking, *These highly experienced, specialized doctors will surely have better ultrasounds and more answers for us.* One question that would not leave my mind was, I*s Karina really due at the end of June or the beginning of August?* The measurements didn't seem right for her to be due on June 30, but my own calculations and the dates of first feeling her move didn't fit with me not being due until August 6.

Excerpt from CarePages

June 5, 2007

The mass on her face looks much bigger than it did with the other ultrasounds. There is no definite place that it is coming from. We can see her eyes and her nose and then it's just a blur. We don't know where it starts or goes, but thankfully, it doesn't seem to affect her vertebrae in her neck. The specialists could not tell us her chance of survival or if the tumor would be able to be removed, as it depends on how it is attached. The verse for today is from Psalm 48:10: Be still and know that I am God" (ESV).

In Christ,
Christie for the Geaschels

Over time, none of the doctors who we visited wanted me to go into labor on my own. They thought that the dark area that they saw was probably a tumor or teratoma. If it blocked her airway, Karina might not be able to breathe once she was born. Because of this, the surgeon would need a very experienced Pediatric ENT (Ear, Nose, and Throat) surgeon in the delivery room to help establish an airway. The maternal-fetal doctors thought that a planned delivery might be her only chance for survival, and only if the right specialists were ready. Although they knew so much, these doctors were perplexed by what they saw on the ultrasounds.

We met most of the staff at that maternal-fetal clinic, and I felt like a celebrity when I called them. One day when I called the office, I left my name, and a doctor, whom I had only met once, said, "Oh, I know who you are, but you probably don't know me." I was not used to that. The specialists saw so many patients every day and every year, that in my experience, it usually took a while for them to get to know new patients, but in our case, it was different.

After visiting with the maternal-fetal doctors a couple of times and having more ultrasounds and non-stress tests, they determined we needed to go to a more-specialized university hospital. After checking with Madison and Chicago, they sent us to Prentice Women's Hospital, which was affiliated with Northwestern University in downtown Chicago.

2

"WHAT DO YOU THINK ABOUT Philly?" It was the first time that we had met our new obstetrics doctor (OB), and he was not sure if he had the capability to perform the delivery at his hospital. Upon hearing his question, Bill and I looked at each other and laughed.

I thought back over the past couple of weeks. I had gone from a planned home birth to a hospital birth, to a high-risk hospital birth, to a probable C-section, to a C-section in downtown Chicago, to a possible C-section in Philadelphia. I wondered, *What next?* This doctor told us that they delivered ten thousand babies a year at Northwestern Hospital, yet they hadn't seen anything similar to this in five years. He had to do some checking around and find out if it was possible for their hospital to handle Karina's complex delivery.

Again, we felt like we were being treated like celebrities. The three nurses in the OB-GYN department at Prentice prayed with us for Karina and the upcoming delivery. They knew it was safe to pray with us after we had explained what the baby was named and that we were trusting God with her little life. They were so eager to join us in prayer and thrilled to have fellow believers in their office.

The next week, we went back for a second appointment. This time, the OB doctor assured us that he would find a way to help us and that he wouldn't send us out of state. He had to find a pediatric ENT from Children's Memorial Hospital who could get surgery rights at Northwestern Hospital. That way, the Pediatric ENT could be at the delivery to establish an airway for Karina if she couldn't breathe upon delivery.

We had more ultrasounds and met more doctors. They all felt that the baby was not due quite yet but that we probably did not have much time. I also had many non-stress tests because Karina seemed to be sleeping at every appointment. They wanted to make sure that she was moving and that her heart rate was changing as it was supposed to. Thankfully, they let me have most of the ultrasounds and non-stress tests (NST) in Rockford, so we did not have to travel to Chicago quite so often. At most of my appointments, I'd have to drink Pepsi to assure that she would wake up and move during the tests.

One day as I was driving to one of the appointments, Karina moved constantly. I was eager to get to the appointment so that the nurses would trust that she was active. It ended up taking so long in the waiting room that by the time I saw the physician and then went for the ultrasound, she once again was sound asleep.

After a couple of weeks, we went back to Chicago to have an MRI. It would help the doctors determine the size of Karina's tumor and figure out exactly where it was located. As we were preparing for the MRI, the doctors reluctantly informed us that if Karina's airway was blocked, there was nothing that they could do to help her. From what the tests showed, the tumor was about the size of a small grapefruit or an orange at this point, and Karina weighed about four pounds.

After arriving home from Chicago, I again posted on CarePages.

June 22, 2007

Dear praying family and friends,

Thank you, thank you, thank you for your prayers. Yesterday, Karina passed her non-stress test better than she had any time in the past! I also got the second of my steroid shots to help her lung development. Today we (my parents, the kids, Bill, and I) were up bright and early and on the road by 6:15 a.m. We got to the MRI place at 8:00 a.m., and we were done by 9:15 a.m.

Karina did great for the MRI. I had to be on a twelve-hour fast so that she would not be too active, and she lay very still. After we finished, we waited around patiently until the radiologist came in with the much-anticipated MRI reading. She said that there is still some opening in Karina's airway (Praise the Lord!). After that, I had an ultrasound on Karina's mass. Then we again sat and waited to talk to the pediatric ENT. The ENT said he doesn't want us to wait much longer to deliver, and Bill and I also feel that it will be in Karina's best interests if she is delivered soon. Right now, her airway is still open, but we don't know at what point it might not be.

The kids spent the morning at the Lincoln Park Zoo with my parents, and we joined them via cab around noon. Now that we know that Karina still has an airway to work with, I hope to sleep much better tonight.

Thank you again for your prayers.

In Christ,
Christie for the family

Imagine leaving home at 6:15 a.m. with two senior citizens, a dad, a pregnant and scared mom, and seven children, ranging in ages from fifteen months to eleven years old. The children had gone to bed early the night before, with the clothing that they would wear the next day already on them. They were all in bright yellow shirts, and the girls were in denim skirts and jumpers so that they could easily be counted and seen by their grandparents at the zoo.

Breakfast, lunch, and snacks had been packed up for the daylong journey, and the diaper bag was packed with changes of clothes and diapers for the youngest child. The double stroller was put into the van, as well as all my medical notes and notebooks that I took with me to every appointment. It was a lot of work for the whole family to be gone from our home for the day, but we tried to include everyone as often as we could and make it as fun as we could.

That day, the tests that I had at the hospital were interesting. I was having the tests done at Children's Memorial Hospital so that the pediatric ENT could see the condition of Karina, his soon-to-be patient. The only way to see her and find out her needs was to do an ultrasound and an MRI on her mommy.

I remember feeling embarrassed as I was gowned, prepped, and tested at the children's hospital because the oldest patient was almost twenty years younger than I was. I also wondered how many times other mothers had been tested at children's hospitals for the sake of their soon-to-be-born babies.

We were very impressed with Children's Memorial Hospital, as the staff was friendly and helpful, and the hallways and rooms were clean, colorful, fun, and inviting.

As soon as the tests were over and we had spoken with all the doctors that we needed to see, Bill and I, feeling very relieved, headed out to the closest street to find a taxi. It had been our first visit to Children's Memorial Hospital, our first taxi ride, and a wonderful afternoon at the Lincoln Park Zoo with the family.

During the next weeks before the delivery, we had to keep in contact with all the doctors and keep everyone up to date. Frequently, the ENT and the OB doctor talked. As it got closer to my new August due date, the doctors decided that they wanted to take Karina by C-section about three weeks early.

We had a lot to do before then. We met the anesthesiologist so that she could go over everything with us about the things that we could expect during the delivery procedure. She explained all the extreme examples of things that could go wrong, and how the whole surgery would be performed. She told me that I would have to be asleep for the C-section. That way, she could make sure that my whole body was at rest and there wasn't any chance of contractions causing problems for the surgeon. She also told me that, unfortunately, Bill would not be able to be in the room during the delivery.

We also met with another OB doctor from Prentice Women's Hospital, who was going to be the one performing the C-section. I had another ultrasound because she needed to know exactly where the placenta was, and she wanted to mark on my belly with a permanent marker, to make sure that the placenta was not in the way of the C-section. During the delivery, they would first bring out Karina's head and torso so that the ENT could establish an airway. Then they would deliver the rest of her body. The placenta could not be disturbed; otherwise, they would run out of time to help Karina get an airway before she would need to breathe. This was a unique procedure, which was called EXIT (ex utero intrapartum treatment) procedure, and it was only done about five times a year in the United States.

Lastly, while we were in Chicago, we met the neonatal physician. He would be at the delivery, as well, to care for Karina after the ENT was done making sure that she had an open airway. He gave us a tour of Northwestern NICU's nursery, where she would be until she transferred to Children's Memorial Hospital. We were relieved to learn that he also worked at Children's Memorial and that he would have his rotation there a few weeks after Karina was scheduled to be born.

3

"AFTER SURGERY, I DON'T KNOW what we are going to find. I don't know how long I will be away from my kids. I need them with me these last few days before the delivery, " I explained to the receptionist, who was making arrangements for us to stay in Chicago for the few days before the scheduled delivery.

As it got closer to my delivery date, the doctors were adamant about me not going into labor at home. However, if that were to happen, they told me to call emergency services for an ambulance or helicopter. They also decided to put my family and parents up in a Chicago hotel for a few days prior to the delivery date. Our accommodations were located on Michigan Avenue and within walking distance of shops, dining, the beach, and a playground.

The hospital staff was only going to provide a place for Bill and me to stay, but I told them that I needed my kids with me. So instead of Bill and me staying alone, all seven kids and my parents joined us. We relished our time together. One day we went to the beach, and the night before the delivery we went out for a Chicago-style pizza supper.

Our suite was more like an apartment than hotel rooms. It had a kitchen, two bedrooms, and a bathroom. Our youngest children were delighted that they could sit in the window seat while they looked out onto the sidewalk and the playground. There was also an area in the suite where we could play games, sit, and talk.

The fenced-in playground was directly across the street from our accommodations. It was a stress-release to be able to spend time playing with and enjoying my children and not having to constantly think about the upcoming birth and the things that it might entail. It was relieving to me that they had this meaningful family time because most of their summer had been interrupted by appointments, Chicago trips, and various babysitters.

When we walked under the expressway and down a couple of blocks, we could play in the waves of Lake Michigan Beach and build sandcastles together. The youngest girls were content playing in the sand with their little buckets and shovels. As I was still a few weeks from my due date, I was feeling great physically. I treasured the moments that we spent together, as I had no idea what we would encounter on the other side of the delivery.

I had sent emails and texts, asking friends and family members to help with the children in the upcoming weeks, as I did not really know how long I would be away. Meals as well as practical help and care for the children were specifically on my mind. It was important to know who was going to be at our house and at what time they would be there, as none of the children were old enough to be left alone.

The morning of the delivery, the surgeons and their university shadows practiced the upcoming EXIT delivery with a baby doll at 4:30 a.m. They had never performed anything like it, and the forty-plus doctors, nurses, and other staff members needed to figure out where they were going to stand, the order of events that would occur, and the temperature of the room. The OB surgeon wanted the temperature cool for the delivery, but the pediatrician wanted it warm for Karina's sake. Later, we were informed that there had been so many people crammed into the operating room that at one point, the surgeon said strictly, "Anyone who doesn't have to be in the room, please leave."

So that Bill and my parents could be at the hospital during the delivery, my cousin, who lives in Chicago, took the day off work and came to stay with our children. We were feeling sad, but also excited and eager, as we left the kids that morning, not knowing what was going to happen during the delivery. I had been told of the chances of Karina's survival and my chances of complications and hemorrhaging with the prolonged C-section. We prayed with our family, gave our many hugs and kisses, and then left for the hospital, just a few short blocks away.

Our pastor joined us for the day, to pray with us and to sit with Bill and my parents during the delivery. Bill's brother, also a pastor, came for the big day, as well.

Shortly before the nurses wheeled me out of the room for the surgery, the head nurse approached me and asked for my permission to take photos during the surgery, for the benefit of future medical classes. I did give her permission on the condition that she also used my camera, as Bill could not be in the delivery room, and I had to be asleep. I realized afterward, when looking back at the whole Chicago experience, that I had become bolder.

After saying my goodbyes to my parents and Bill, along with more hugs, kisses, prayers, and a few tears, I was wheeled out of the room, down a long hall, and into the operating room where I was met with a sea of faces.

Physically, it was cold and sterile. Everyone scurried around and busily prepared for that uncommon delivery. I had never seen so many doctors and nurses in one room before. I did not recognize anyone because they were all fully attired for the surgery.

I was sure that they could imagine my unease in this unique situation. I could see by the creases in their eyes, when they would smile at me from behind their masks, that they were trying to comfort me.

I was very apprehensive about getting the epidural. I do not like needles, and the idea of a huge one in my back was not something that I wanted to ponder. After the needle had been inserted, the anesthesiologist's nurse came and put my oxygen mask over my mouth and nose to put me to sleep. I could not handle it. It was too much! I felt claustrophobic and grabbed at the mask. I told her I could not breathe, and she reluctantly pulled it away. I do not remember the next events. Somehow, they found another way to put me to sleep.

I woke up in the recovery room, and of course, I instantly wondered how Karina was. The nurses informed me that the delivery had gone well and that the ENT had intubated her, which meant that she had a breathing tube. She would be fed through a tube in her nose (NG tube), and she had countless wires hooked up to her belly button.

The nurse mentioned that the tumor was huge and that it made her look chubby, even though she was only five pounds five ounces. She also told me that Karina looked very alert. Lastly, I was informed that I could not leave the recovery room until I could move my legs. I remember lying there, looking at my feet and toes sticking up like mountains under the blankets, and wondering why I could not move them. I kept trying, but they just would not budge. I tried harder, thinking that if I just wanted it badly enough, they would move, but instead, I had to wait until the medications wore off enough before my legs would begin to work again.

When I was finally able to see Bill, he told me that Karina was going by ambulance to Children's Memorial Hospital later that day. I really wanted to see her first and I knew it would be important for her siblings to be able to see her too. I knew that I would have to stay at the hospital for at least the next couple of days. Oh, how I wanted to see and hold my dear baby Karina Faith.

As soon as I was stable enough to leave the recovery room, they wheeled me, while I lay in my recovery room bed, all the way to the nursery so that I could attempt to see our newest baby girl. I was not able to sit up yet, so I was barely able to reach my arm out to touch her little fingers and toes and see her face. I knew that it would be a long couple of days until I could go to Children's Memorial Hospital to be with her. Oh, how deeply I wanted to tell her that it was going to be OK and that I loved her. Being two arm's lengths away (my arm and her arm) just was not the same.

I wondered how often the large mommas' beds had been wheeled into the small nursery so that the moms could get a look at their babies, who could not be moved from the isolette. I figured this was not a common occurrence, and I was thankful that they let me get that close. I was also so thankful to God that she was OK and that these physicians had been trained for emergencies such as this. They could help when things were not normal and when babies could not be delivered in the comfort of a home, or even a normal hospital birth.

The time came when Karina would be transferred to Children's Memorial Hospital. My dad was called, inviting him to bring the four oldest kids, aged 11, 9, 8, and 6, to come quickly to the hospital and see Karina before she left. They left on foot from the hotel and hurried through downtown Chicago until they reached the hospital. The little group went to the nursery's floor just in time to see Karina Faith in her little enclosed isolette being wheeled to the awaiting ambulance.

I encouraged Bill to go with Karina, as I knew I was OK. She needed someone to go with her and speak for her. Bill rode across town in the ambulance with Karina and her special nurses. Then he stayed a few hours until she was settled in a room in the NICU.

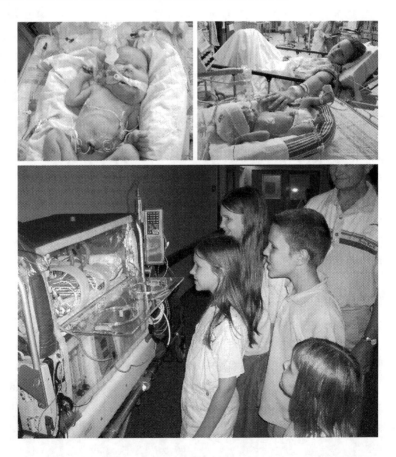

Later that day, my parents brought all of our kids to the hospital, so they were able to come up to my room and see me. They were excited to all be together, but little Elaina, who was four years old at the time, was heartbroken when she saw me in bed. She really wanted me to come back with them to the hotel. In her distress, tears streamed down her face.

On the day after the delivery when my OB doctor came to check on me, she told me that the delivery had gone even better than they had planned. She informed me that EXIT procedure deliveries normally took anywhere from fifteen minutes to two hours. The time between Karina's head coming out and the rest of her body being delivered only took six minutes! During that time, they had put in a tube so that she could breathe, secured it so that it wouldn't be dislodged in any way, and made sure that she could breathe with it, before they had finished the rest of the delivery.

I had heard that things went well, but I had not been made aware how quickly it had all taken place. Praise the Lord! He had helped us find the right specialists who could help Karina through her unique entrance into the world.

The OB surgeon only made me stay two days after the delivery, but those days were a blur. I do not remember eating, writing and posting on the CarePages, talking on the phone with friends and loved ones, pumping (expressing) milk for Karina, or getting my strength up to be able to walk, shower, and put my clothes on. I must have done all those things because when I got the discharge paperwork, I was ready.

I immediately called the Ronald McDonald House (RMH) to secure a room so that Bill and I could move directly over there from Prentice. I was surprised to learn that they were full for the night. Since Bill and I could not get into the RMH right away, we spent a few nights at Children's Memorial Hospital in a parent-waiting room. The room we were given was small, with only a couple of recliners, a sofa and a small coffee table with magazines on top of it. It was close to the NICU rooms, and many parents would use it throughout the day to rest in between their infant visits and cuddles.

On arriving at Children's Memorial Hospital, my main goal was to get Karina's surgery scheduled so that they could remove the awful tumor, and we could go home and rejoin our other children.

Excerpt from CarePages

July 16, 2007

Dear family and friends,

I'm sorry that my communications to you have been few and far between. We keep waiting for word when Karina's surgery will take place. I am getting stronger, although I have to keep up with my pain medicine; otherwise, my incision is still really sore. I have also overcome the bloating of surgery, although I am now dealing with swollen ankles and feet, things I did not know that can happen with a C-section.

Bill started pushing me around yesterday (in a wheelchair, of course), so I am able to rest much more. I also got to see my nurses and one of the OB doctors again today, in order to get my staples removed. Pumping was going really well when Karina was given five milliliters of my milk every three hours, but now they upped it to fifteen milliliters every three hours. As hard as I try, I can't do it. I am pumping what I can, and they supplement it with formula (the issue of not having enough milk tended to be a struggle for me with most of my babies).

We get to feed Karina my milk and the formula through her feeding tube. I have also gotten to change her diapers. We don't get to hold her yet because of her airway tube. It's still too risky. It might come out of her airway. She is getting much more alert. She knows when we are in the room. Her blood pressure starts to go up if she can't see us or feel our touch, but knows we are there in the room.

When that happened this morning, the nurse turned off her bilirubin lights and took off her little mask. Right away, she opened her eyes and calmed down. Her blood pressure returned to normal, and she just kept looking at us. I was amazed that such a young infant could understand so much. We stood there talking and singing to Karina for a short time, and then the nurses had a shift change, so we had to leave the room, which was hard to do.

This will be our third night staying at Children's Hospital. We keep thinking that we will get into a RMH room, but it hasn't happened yet. I haven't minded, though. Our room is right next to Karina's, so if I wake up at 4:00 a.m., 5:00 a.m., or whenever, I can pop in and see her.

Please keep us in your prayers. Karina still has a risky surgery coming up sometime soon. We will do our best to keep in touch.

Love,
Christie and Bill

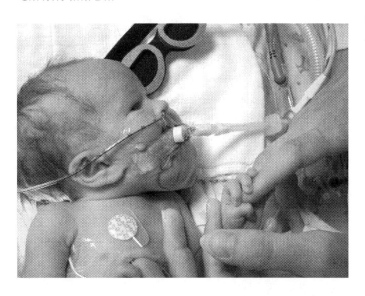

Excerpt From Carepages

Update to July 16, 2007 Later that night,

Well, things changed drastically. We thought we still had a room at the hospital, but they booked someone in around us, so at seven tonight, we decided to head home. We needed clean clothes anyway, and I wanted to see the kids.

While Bill was packing up our stuff, I got a phone call from the lady who was trying to get some publicity for us. WGN News wants to cover our story, and they want to film us in Chicago tomorrow, with the kids! So we are at home refreshing ourselves, getting sleep in a bed, sending this update, and then heading back to Chicago in the morning with the kids and grandparents in tow. Please pray that we can be a witness through our story and that they won't cut out the important parts. We will let you know when it airs.

We also found out that Karina will probably have some kind of biopsy done on her tumor before surgery is scheduled. The surgeons want to be very certain what is involved with this delicate procedure before they cut into it. If it is too vascular (involving veins), there will be major problems because of possibly too much bleeding. Now that I understand what we are waiting for, it's easier to be patient. The mom in me just wants that awful thing out of my baby's mouth.

Good night.

Love,
Christie

The big event of the next day was that WGN News came to interview our family. Prentice Women's Hospital wanted publicity for the new procedure that they performed during Karina's delivery. We consented, and we were hoping to be a witness of God's love and faithfulness through our situation.

We felt good about the interview when it was finished. We had made it clear that God was the reason that Karina was doing well and that she was even alive. We were sure our faith-in-God theme would be so interwoven throughout the interview that there would be no possible way to remove it.

4

"THAT WAS NOT AT ALL what we expected!" I told Bill. "They cut out everything that we said about our faith and how God has helped us through the past six-plus weeks, since finding out about Karina's mass."

We were glad that we had the opportunity, but it sure did not play out as we had expected. During the interview, the reporters talked to the OB doctor, the ENT, and other specialists. Then they interviewed Bill and me. Our seven oldest children all sat around a table that was in the center courtyard of the hospital, playing with Play-Doh. It was a good way to keep them in one area while still filming them all together.

When the WGN News interview aired, we realized that they had utilized only the portions they wanted to get across their agenda and to eliminate our desire to praise God through the interview. Their agenda was only to give their hospital some publicity. It said, "Look what we can do." Our agenda was to convey, "Look what God did." Since they were the ones with the editors and cameras, their agenda won.

Excerpt from Carepages

July 17, 2007

Wow! What a day it was. See if you can experience the emotional roller coaster that we were on today.

- *It started at 6:00 a.m., when we got up and prepared for the big day.*
- *I weighed myself while I was at home. I actually gained weight after delivering (Now do you understand how big my legs and feet are?) I would have laughed if my muscles hadn't been so sore.*
- *We received a call that we will get into a room at RMH, beginning tonight.*
- *The ENT let us know that Karina will not be having surgery at this time to remove her tumor. But she will go into surgery tomorrow afternoon for a tracheostomy.*
- *The other ENT will also do a biopsy during the same surgery to determine if the tumor is malignant. If it is, they will remove it soon. If it is not, they may wait as long as six months before they remove it. They want to give her time to grow.*
- *We might be able to go home as soon as two to three weeks, if everything goes well with the tracheostomy.*
- *I got to hold Karina for the first time today.*
- *We were interviewed by WGN News.*
- *Gramps and Grandma Coco and Grandma Judy got to see Karina today.*

- *We took the kids to the hospital's playroom. They had a lot of fun. They all went home with prizes from a bingo game.*
- *Elaina asked me many times if she could see Karina.*
- *We met with a family life specialist, who showed the kids a doll with a tracheostomy and read them a book about how to care for a baby with trach. They learned not to poke anything into it.*
- *I had to say goodbye to my kids tonight before they went home. I miss them so much. Please pray for my emotional state and Karina's surgery tomorrow.*

Love,
Christie

The doctors' decision to put in a tracheostomy instead of intubating Karina was a tough one for me to accept. It seemed to be such a life-altering procedure. I just wanted us to go home, but when they talked about putting in the trach, it felt like they were telling me that my baby was not going home for a long time. With intubation, I knew that it was temporary, and she would have to have it taken out before too much longer, which meant that the surgery would be soon, and we would be going home.

After much thought and prayer, we eventually accepted the idea of a tracheostomy. We also gave the ENT permission to take videos and photos during the procedure for his cross-country lectures. I told him that we believed that God had brought us there for a purpose and that if we could help the doctors in any way, we would love to.

Before she went into surgery, we were able to hold Karina again. It was so wonderful to be able to hold my baby again and feel like she was mine and not the nurses'. Holding her was cumbersome because she had so many tubes and wires connecting her to the monitors and machines.

After I was sitting in a rocking chair, a nurse would hand her to me, and then they would arrange all of her wires and tubes.

Along with the blood pressure, oxygen, and heart-rate monitor wires, she also had a humidifier hooked up to her breathing tube and an NG tube in her nose. There was also something attached to her belly button, which they could use to draw or give blood through, as needed.

I held Karina as long as they would allow, as I knew that I would not be able to do so again for another week after the surgery.

During her surgery, they took the first biopsy, tissue from the tumor, and sent it to a lab to determine what the tumor really was.

After they put in the tracheostomy, the ENTs kept her sedated for a few days so that the trach hole could heal. Karina could not be weighed or moved for any reason, but I was allowed to start giving her a pacifier. Now she could have something pleasant in her mouth occasionally. I did not like that the awful-looking, foul-smelling tumor was hanging out of my baby's mouth. At least with the pacifier, she could do something enjoyable with her tongue.

Once they had put in the tracheostomy, it was so wonderful to finally see her face! She still had the NG tube hooked up through her nose for feedings, but we could finally see her mouth and cheeks without all the tape they had used for the intubation tube.

Bill stayed with me through the first week after the delivery, and then my mom stayed with me the second week. After that, I would be on my own. It was the same daily routine. I waited to bring our youngest baby home.

Twice during that first two weeks, I was asked by two different people when my baby was due. "Well," I would tell them, "she was born a couple of weeks ago." It was awkward! I knew that my bloating was severe enough that I looked like I was still pregnant. I was currently wearing my maternity clothes because nothing else that I owned fit. My legs and ankles were also so swollen that I had to buckle my sandals on the last hole. Usually, my feet were very thin and bony.

At some point during most weekends, Bill and the kids would come for a visit. I loved those days and greatly enjoyed some diversion from the monotonous schedule that I was on during the week.

Excerpt from CarePages

July 29, 2007

We had a great day together today. The four oldest kids got to hold Karina for the first time. The younger ones got to see her, except for Jena (sixteen months old), who doesn't even know she has a sister. We spent some time playing in the hospital playroom, and then we went to the RMH for the rest of the day.

For our lunch, Bill brought in leftovers from some of the delicious meals that friends have been bringing for the family. We played outside at the RMH. Around 3:00 p.m., some volunteers came. They helped the kids make brownies, decorate them, and then they ate them. After that, we had supper, which more volunteers brought in. Britta and Eva helped me get my laundry done. We also let the kids play in the RMH playroom, before they all went home at around 7:30 p.m., and I went back to the hospital.

As I had the same nurse as on Friday night, I again got to bathe and dress Karina in the preemie clothes that I had brought to the hospital, change her trach collar, and clean out her trach. In the morning, Bill is planning to get everyone up very early, get them all ready for church, and then come and get me. We will hopefully make it to church by 10:30 a.m. We'll see how it goes.

Thank you for your continued prayers. I am looking forward to finally being able to let you all know what Karina has in her mouth and the plans of what they will do with it. The news should come Monday or Tuesday. Also, now that I am going to be alone here, I'd love to have visitors. Adults and kids who are fourteen and older can also visit Karina. For now, good night.

-Christie

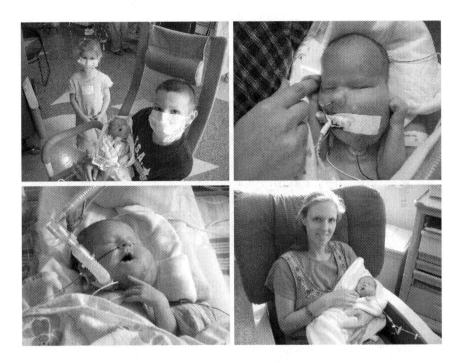

That day at the Ronald McDonald House (RMH) was so much fun. We felt like a normal family again for a few hours. The playroom was so colorful and vibrant, with bright pictures on the walls, shelves of toys, and piles of stuffed animals. The kids liked to dress up as cowboys or Buzz Lightyear. Then they went outside and rode bikes and played with balls.

The RMH was a wonderful place to be while staying in Chicago. There were two kitchens, and that afternoon, we had the whole basement kitchen to ourselves. We heated up our food and ate together.

The weekend visits kept me going through the week because I missed my family so much. Each time they would leave, Elaina would start crying and once again tell me, "I thought you were coming home this time." Usually, I would start crying too. I tried to console her as well as I could, but it was trying on all of us. Even though I longed to go home, I knew that being with Karina was the place that I needed to be at that time. The other children could be together as family members and friends cared for them. Karina needed me to be with her and learning all that I could about taking care of her.

The Sunday that Bill and the kids picked me up was a rare treat. They left the house around 6:00 a.m. and came to get me. On the way to church, I plugged the breast pump into an outlet converter in the van and covered myself with blankets so that I could pump and have milk to bring back to the hospital for Karina's evening feeding.

I also had to pump while I was at church because it had already been another three hours. At the church building, I brought a chair into a cold, tiny back room, which also held a water heater. The chair and I barely fit in that little room. I was not very relaxed, but I did my pumping for Karina's sake. I then put my small amounts of milk in a cooler to bring back to the hospital for the nurses to add to her next feeding.

As Karina took in more and more at her feedings, the amount that I was pumping seemed smaller and smaller. It was the best that I could do for her at that time, and I was determined to pump as long as I could.

"Hurry up and wait," became my motto each day, as I rushed to the hospital to get news and discovered that there was no news yet. That was the situation on July 30. I hurried to the hospital in the morning around 7:30 a.m. and waited for the news. Finally at 4:00 p.m., I received the long awaited news that we had been anticipating for the previous twelve days: There was no news yet. The pathologists were all very confused. The tumor did not look like any of the three types of tumors that biopsies usually showed. So they were back to the beginning. After sending out two sets of biopsied material, the pathologists were doing another cutting of the second biopsy that evening. At that point, all I could ask for was prayer for the doctors to have wisdom and discernment. I also needed patience.

CHAPTER

5

"IT'S AMAZING WHAT SOME PRAYER and a good night's sleep can accomplish" I woke up and posted on CarePages, with a new day and a new perspective.

First, I was thankful that Karina was doing well. She was off all life support. She was growing, peaceful and content. The tumor did not seem to bother her or be growing.

Second, I realized that I had been trying to rush God's plan. He knew that we were both there in Chicago, and He wanted us to be there. He had a reason for it. When He was ready for us to go home, we would. I woke up and thought, *I feel ready to meet the day and whatever the Lord brings.*

It was so much more complicated caring for Karina than it had been for our other babies. She made no sounds. With the tracheostomy, her coughs and sneezes sounded identical. Unless we were watching her facial expressions or her blood pressure, we did not know if she was happy, sad, crying, or mad. She had only been able to show expression on one side of her face since she had had her tracheostomy when she was one week old.

I wondered if something had happened during her tracheostomy surgery or the biopsy. Maybe the lack of expression was caused by the tumor pressing on her nerves. We did not know if we would ever find the cause.

Karina did not like to be hungry or have a dirty diaper. Her blood pressure would go up, and the right side of her face would look distressed. As soon as her situation was improved, she would be restful and spend most of her time sleeping.

During much of the time that I spent in her room each day, I would stand by her crib (or sit on a high stool), hold her hands, and talk to her. I would also talk to the nurses and the other parents in the room. I always wanted to know why the nurses were doing what they were doing and the reason that Karina's monitors were doing what they were doing. I wanted to understand as much as I could because my desire was to care for Karina at home and not to be in the hospital long term.

I could not sit in the rockers as the other moms did because if I did, I couldn't see Karina, and she couldn't see me. I did not even hold her very often, even though I was with her most of each day. It was complicated to hold her, and she seemed much more comfortable in her bed.

On Tuesday of that week, I was invited to a mom's scrapbooking session at the hospital. I met a few other moms at the scrapping event. I was given a small Creative Memories scrapbook, and all the materials that I wanted, and two hours to work on the book. The table was full of every color of paper, stickers, punches, markers, and stencils imaginable. We were invited to come back every Tuesday, but all of us moms agreed that although we enjoyed the time to work on the books, we longed to go home with our babies.

Excerpt from CarePages

August 3, 2007

Hi, all. Not much has changed, except for the fact that Bill is here. He is starting to learn how to care for Karina and her equipment, for the time when we will get the word that we can go home. He now understands why I really pray that we don't have to go home with the trach. It's hard work changing the ties for it, with her large tumor in the way, and her inability to move her neck makes it that much more challenging. Today we will experience the changing of the trach itself.

Two more slices of biopsy have been sent across the country. One went to Utah. We are praying that the four places the slices were sent to all agree on the same diagnosis.

It's time to head to the hospital. Have a great day.

This is the day that the Lord has made. Let us rejoice and be glad in it (Psalm 118:24 ESV).

Love,
Christie for the Geaschels

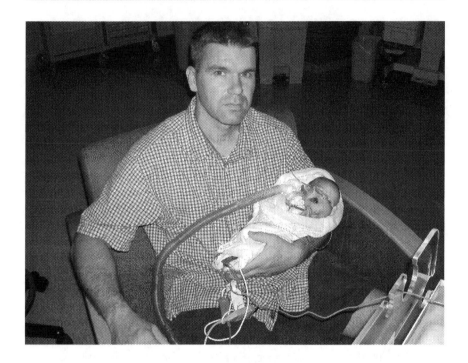

During my weeks in Chicago, I would have to keep a running list of the things that were needed at home, so I could then call my mom to get groceries, toiletries, and other needed items for the family. I also had to keep up with who was staying with the children and who was bringing the evening meals so that Bill could serve them when he arrived home. Sometimes friends came to our house for the day to play with our children. Others took them on outings, usually using our van.

One story I heard happened when the kids spent the day at my brother and sister-in-law's home. After lunch, they were trying to decide what to do next. Britta, who was eleven years old at the time, piped up and said that they should probably do rest time. Armin, who was almost ten, set up the Pack 'n Play and put his youngest sister, Jena, down for a nap. While he was getting that set up, Britta laid a quilt down and set out quiet activities for the other children to work on like knitting and coloring.

My brother joined them on the quilt, and he eventually fell asleep while the children played quietly. Britta and Armin both grew so much that summer. They were great helpers to their little sisters and to the people who helped take care of them.

CHAPTER

6

"FEAR NOT, I AM WITH you, oh be not dismayed, for I am your God and will still give you aid. I'll strengthen you, help you and cause you to stand, upheld by my righteous omnipotent hand" (Rippon, 1990, 612).

As I read these words, I was so thankful for my husband, who had written out some wonderful hymns to help me keep my mind focused on God. I read these words over and over, as my family left to go home after an eventful day.

On August 5, Bill, his parents, and all the kids came to visit me for the day. First, the kids took turns holding Karina. Then, while Grandpa Jim and Grandma Judy stayed with Karina, the rest of us went to the hospital playroom, where we spent time with some therapy dogs. The children enjoyed the dogs and loved that they could get their pictures taken with them. Some of the girls worked on craft projects, and the other children played.

After spending the day together and eating pizza around 8:00 p.m. at the RMH, the family and grandparents brought me back to the hospital at 9:00 p.m., and with feelings of great sadness, my family headed for home. Then I was alone once again, in Chicago with Karina and my God.

Excerpt from CarePages

August 6, 2007

Dear friends and family,

We've had one more day of waiting. I was expecting to talk to the ENT surgeon today, who would tell me what the plan is for surgery. Finally, at 2:00 p.m., the resident that works with the surgeon came in and said that the ENT was in surgery and that he would come and talk to me in an hour. So I sat by Karina's bed and waited. At 4:40 p.m., the resident and the ENT came, met with me and the neonatologist, and told us that they did not have a plan yet. They have to wait until the pathologists do more staining of the biopsy scans tonight. He will talk with me tomorrow.

The tumor has everyone stumped. It appears to be a fibrous lesion, but that is not very defining. It could be one of many things. Each one would have to be removed in a very different way. A malignancy is not totally out of the question yet either. It sounds like there still might be another MRI or ultrasound in the near future also, unless I misunderstood them.

I am holding up very well. I know that you are all praying for me; otherwise, I could be very emotional about all this. Karina is three and a half weeks old today, and this would have been her due date.

Here is my normal day. Get up in the morning and pump. Then I get myself ready for the day, go to the hospital, drop off the milk from the previous night, and eat breakfast. Then I go see Karina for a while, and it's soon time to pump again. After that, I see Karina for a bit and then go eat lunch. Not long after lunch, it's time to pump again, and then I go back to Karina's room. I hang out there with her and her nurses until it's time to pump again. Then I go back into Karina's room. For supper I eat in the hospital or at the RMH. Then I need to pump again.

Around 8:30 p.m., I go to Karina's room, give her a bath, change her trach ties, and hold her for a while until she calms down as this is emotionally draining for both of us. Then around 9:30 or 10:00, I get a shuttle and go back to the RMH, where I once again pump, update CarePages for you, call Bill to tell him good night, and then go to bed. That's what a day looks like here.

Good night.

Love,
Christie

I can do all things through him who strengthens me. (Phil. 4:13 ESV)

My time in Chicago was a time in my life when I felt most alone. I am not normally comfortable being alone, and it was a very stretching time for me. I was alone at the RMH. I was alone in the small room when I pumped numerous times a day. I was alone as I ate in the cafeteria (Sure, it was full of people, but I rarely ate with any of them). I was alone while walking to the hospital or waiting for the shuttle twice a day. I know that God was with me, and He helped me through those weeks. My faith in Him was increased during that time. It was such an important time in my life, as I learned to be dependent on Him and not on my family and friends.

One day, I went into the RMH's parlor for a much-needed massage. Students from the massage therapy school would offer free massages to the parents who were staying there.

I really did not want a young man to massage me. It was something that I felt strongly about. Each day, I waited and checked the names on the dry-erase board to see who was scheduled to do the massages. Some days, I could not tell by the name if it was a male or female. Other days, it was more obvious.

When I got to the parlor, I was relieved, because Angel was doing the massages. I decided this was my day to get some relief for my shoulders and my back. I turned the corner and went into the parlor. A young man walked over and offered his hand in a handshake, saying, "Hello, I'm Angel [An-hel]." Oh, what did I do? Well, I did not want to leave and be rude, so I told Angel that I just needed my shoulders and upper back massaged. That was my last massage at RMH.

7

"I AM NOT AFRAID OF this surgery. Karina is here for a purpose; otherwise, I would have gone ahead with my home birth, and she might not have made it. God has a plan for her. That's why she is still here. We have witnessed so many miracles along the way, and we know that God is in control." I was talking to the nurses, as the ENT had just left the room. He had told us that he would do the surgery as early as Friday but that it would be a very challenging surgery. Karina would also be having another CT scan before then, and in the meantime, more biopsy stains were sent to Utah.

On August 8, it was my birthday, and my family and parents came to spend the day with me. We went to the Rain Forest Cafe, and we rode on the hospital shuttle and a city bus. Everyone enjoyed the trip, except for Greta (age three), who could not be convinced that the elephants at the Rain Forest Cafe were not real. The restaurant gave us the feeling of walking into a jungle. The animated animals were such fun to watch, and most of the children enjoyed looking at them.

I remember noticing how much my children had changed while I had been away from them. I realized that Armin, our only son, had taken on the responsibility of keeping track of his sisters. While all of the girls watched the fish swimming around in the huge aquarium, he stayed fifteen-to-twenty feet back so that he could watch over all of his little sisters. It was a heartwarming experience for me to watch him.

The kids gave me a wonderful surprise for my birthday. They had memorized almost the entire Psalm 139! A friend, who had been caring for them weekly, had a recording of it that had been put to music, and she taught them so that they could sing it for me. We were in my room at RMH. I sat on the bed, and they all started singing. It was wonderful!

Back at the hospital, Bill and I met with the ENT surgeon once more. As he told us- multiple times- what a difficult surgery it would be, he said, "If she makes it through surgery." We had full confidence in God, knowing that He was in control no matter what the outcome of the surgery on Friday was. We did not know of any other way to get our baby home.

On August 9, 2007, after weeks of tests and waiting, more tests and waiting, and biopsies being sent out multiple times, it was the long-awaited night before surgery. We had friends and relatives preparing to join us the next day while we waited for the tumor to be removed. I spent the evening holding Karina's hands, talking to her, and praying to God. There were tears in my eyes as I thought about the next day's big event.

CHAPTER

8

"THE SURGERY IS OFF. IF I do that surgery tomorrow, she won't make it off the operating table. Let's try oncology." I couldn't believe what I had just heard. I had been sitting on a high stool in my normal spot next to Karina, just talking to her, and thinking about the next day's surgery, when the surgeon walked in and started talking to me. I had turned around so that I could better talk with him, when he gave the shattering news.

As the surgeon walked out of the room, my mind was spinning. *What? What did he just say? No surgery? We won't be going home? Oncology? They are going to put chemicals into my baby?* Once again, it seemed like a nightmare. I had to call Bill and tell him the news. I also had to let everyone know that they should not come the next day because the surgery was off.

I felt so alone and small. I knew once again, I had to trust God. I typed out my feelings onto the CarePages' network, and I was further encouraged by family and friends who were so helpful to me at that time. They sent me Bible verses, hymns, encouraging words, and prayers. They helped me get through those long days and nights. I was also thankful for the doctor's wisdom. He had felt uneasy enough that he had cancelled the surgery. He later told us that Karina would have lost half of her jaw, that there would have been nerve damage, and that she might have lost a lot of blood, if he had done the surgery.

The ENT surgeon got on the phone and talked with oncology, radiology, pathology, and any other "ologies" that were involved. They decided that chemotherapy would be a much better option for her. Bill decided to come to the hospital immediately, so that we could talk with the oncologists together.

As soon as Bill arrived we met with the specialists. According to the oncologists, the tumor was said to be one of three different kinds of tumors, and one kind could be cancerous. All three tumors would respond to chemo, but different medications would more specifically attack different tumors, and the drugs for the cancerous kinds had more severe side effects than the drugs for the noncancerous tumors.

They also informed us that they could not move ahead until they were 100 percent sure that they knew which tumor Karina had. We were told that by August 20 they should have that answer, and the next day after that, they could start chemo. Her treatments would most likely be three-to-four days on and then twenty-one days off. After the first rotation, she might be able to go home.

It made me very distraught when I found out that we might not be leaving Children's Memorial until the middle to end of September. By the next day, things seemed brighter. I went back to CarePages and updated my seemingly endless emotional roller coaster.

Excerpt from CarePages

August 11, 2007

Today was much better. I guess I just needed an emotional day, and now I am ready to move ahead. As they came by doing their morning rounds, I told the docs that I was not going to sit here for ten days doing nothing.

Here are some of the things that I shared with them from my to-do list:

- *Seeing if Karina can breathe without the trach*
- *If not, getting her to that point*
- *Starting on some speech therapy so that she can eventually eat*
- *Start letting her taste pumped milk. Up to this point, almost everything that has been done to her mouth has been bad. I don't want to continue like this for the next couple of months. If we do, she will have to be reconditioned, and it will be much longer before she can eat by mouth. I want to do all we can now, while we are just sitting here, so that we can go home without home nurses, without the trach, and without the feeding tube.*

It still looks like we will be starting chemotherapy around August 21. Karina can use prayer for her immune system and strength. Pray also that she will be shielded from the bad side effects that come with any chemo drugs. Last night, Karina hit the six-pound mark, and she is about nineteen inches long.

In Christ,
Christie

The next day, our daughter Britta came to stay with me for a few days. I thought that it would be good for both of us. I knew that a lot of burden had been put on her, being the oldest of the kids, and I thought a break would be good for her, and the company would be great for me.

The day nurse let Karina taste some breast milk on her tongue, and she seemed to like it. She kept wiggling her tongue and poking it out from behind the tumor, looking for more. Britta was also able to watch the trach ties being changed and take part in bath time that evening.

Britta stayed until August 14, and we had a great time together. We enjoyed meals together in the hospital cafeteria. She and I did activities at RMH with the volunteers who came in, and we even had time to watch the movie *Shiloh* while Bill was with us.

During the time that Britta was with me, the speech therapist came and started to work with Karina. She also gave her drops of milk to taste, which we knew was welcomed by her little tongue poking out for more. The therapist was so pleased with how well Karina responded to touch on her face. The main struggles for the therapist were in trying to help Karina look up at a midline and getting her to turn her head on her own.

While Karina was in her hospital bed, the nurses and I were the ones who moved and repositioned her a few times a day. When she would lie on her right side, foul-smelling, red-tinged drainage would come out of her mouth and onto her sheets. We also couldn't see her face when she lay on her right side because of the position of her face. It was important to move her from side to side because she couldn't move her head at all on her own.

9

"I'M GOING HOME ON SATURDAY!" I was so excited to write these words on CarePages the evening of August 16. Bill would bring me home while my parents would stay overnight in my room at RMH and watch over Karina during the day for me. I had so much planned for that day. I made a list of what I wanted to accomplish, because I wanted a direction to aim for, even though I knew that not all of it would get done.

I wanted to get the kids' schoolwork organized so that friends and family members could help them start their school year. I planned to get other things cleaned and organized to make it easier for those who were coming into our home and caring for the children. I also wanted to check the kitchen cabinets and toiletries to find out what the family needed and add it to my grocery list. At this point, Karina was five weeks old, and I had only been home a couple of brief times during that time. I was more than ready to visit our home and our children.

My time at home went very quickly, and I only completed a portion of what I really had wanted to do. I got the schoolwork ready for the kids and labeled it with little Post-it Notes: whose homework it was and what they should be doing with it.

I looked through their piles of school materials and books and found ones that would be easy for someone who came in only once in a while to do with them. I did not want anything that took too much prep work or time to implement. I just wanted them to be able to start with math, reading, and various worksheets.

I also packed some new clothes for myself, as I planned to be at Children's for a few more weeks. In between pumping every three hours and spending time holding and reading to my precious children, my list of physical accomplishments seemed minimal.

10

"YOU ARE NEVER GOING TO believe this."

I finished the resident's sentence by saying, "The tumor is not any of the ones they thought it was, right?"

It was true. The new diagnosis was called a Kaposi's Hemangioendotheolioma (a fibrous vascular tumor). Yay! It was not as rare as the other tumors, and it would respond better to chemo.

While we met with the oncology doctors, we talked about what chemo would mean for Karina and the next steps that needed to be taken. Karina was moved to a different floor of the hospital so that the oncology staff could more closely keep watch over her. I did not realize how much that move would affect us.

She finally became our baby. On the fourth floor (oncology floor), the nurses had rounds to do and only checked on their patients every three hours to see if they needed anything. I was now in charge of

Karina's care, and she was mine to care for. It was harder to leave at night and go to the RMH, knowing that there would not be a nurse sitting there right beside her bed 24/7.

I was looking forward to my mom coming in the next day and bringing my daughter Anna (age nine), who was going to stay with me for a few days. My niece also came along for the ride and then went back home with my mom.

Anna and I enjoyed our time together, making crafts, eating together, and having a much-needed mother-daughter bonding time. I was very thankful that she had been able to come and stay with me.

It was not long until the doctors again talked about us taking Karina home. I was relieved because, before that, I had begun to feel like we would never go home. I had not been able to picture her and me living beyond those hospital walls.

Bill and I prepared by taking some tests so that we could take Karina home. We had to be able to care for her on our own for twenty-four hours without any assistance. I also had to pass some nursing tests regarding taking care of her trach and the PICC line, which was used for her chemo drugs.

I am so thankful that I had stayed with Karina as much as I had since her birth. Getting my crash course in nurses' training over the summer helped us prepare to be able to take Karina home to the family. At that time, many children were waiting on one of the upper hospital floors for their home nursing to be lined up so that they could go home. There was a shortage of nurses, and I was going to be permitted to take Karina home without a home nurse. I figured that with the soon-to-be eight children at home being homeschooled, there was enough chaos. We did not need someone else living there.

Excerpt from CarePages

August 21, 2007

Whew! What a day! My mom, my niece, and Anna came in this morning. Anna is staying until tomorrow. She won a prize playing bingo, made some crafts at the hospital and RMH, and helped me with Karina. Now to the big news: Karina and I might be coming home this weekend. This is how things stand as of 10:00 p.m. on Tuesday night (You know that it could change by tomorrow morning).

Tomorrow Karina will have one more CT scan to make sure that there are no other tumors in her little body. Then they are planning to do her chemotherapy. Since no one is 100 percent sure what kind of mass she has, they are going to use a chemo that works for any of the three kinds of tumors. Two of the medicines that they are going to use are only done one day every 21 days. The other chemo drug is done one day every seven days. For this one, a nurse will come to our house to give the drug once a week.

In order to go home this weekend, there are a few things that Bill and I have to do first. We must go to a CPR class, learn to flush Karina's IVs, show that we can totally take care of her trach and feeding tube, and manage her care by ourselves for twenty-four hours. Bill is coming in tomorrow to spend the day and then take Anna home, but we haven't worked out the twenty-four-hour test yet.

As you might imagine, I have so many thoughts going through my head tonight… Are we really going to go home? Can I really take care of her by myself? How is she going to do on the chemo? Even if I can take care of Karina, will I be able to care for the other seven kids and their schooling?

Thank you for being prayer warriors on behalf of Karina and the rest of the family.

Love,
Christie

11

"GO CALL THE ONCOLOGY DOCTORS!" There was fear in her voice as the nurse commanded the oncology resident to get Karina's specialists to attend to the crisis. They, in turn, called the ENT doctors. In just moments, there were six professionals standing around Karina wondering what to do.

It had all started moments earlier, when the oncology resident and I had walked over to Karina's bed to see how she was doing. We both instantly noticed that she was bleeding profusely from her mouth! I got really scared. The resident called the nurse over to suction out the blood, and the bleeding got worse! That was when she commanded him to get the doctors.

When the doctors all came, Bill, Anna, and I rushed out of the room and went into another small, vacant room to pray. I was so afraid that she was going to bleed to death. Once again, I felt so small and knew that God was the only one who could help her. She was in His hands, and no one else could take care of her like He could.

After about twenty minutes (which seemed like an eternity), the resident came to find us and told us that the bleeding had stopped, as they had packed her mouth with gauze. The doctors told us that since the tumor was vascular, it should respond well to the chemo drugs. This was one time that I was thankful for the trach. Otherwise, either the bleeding or packing her mouth with gauze would have made it difficult for her to breathe.

My theory on the bleeding was that it had started because she was so upset. Earlier in the day, she was supposed to have a CT scan. The nurses stopped her feedings at midnight, and finally at 10:00 a.m., she was wheeled down for the scan. At 10:45 a.m., she bled a small amount from her mouth, and they decided to wait on the scan. By 11:30 a.m., she was back in her room, but her feeding tube had come out, so they went to find another one. Because we were on a new floor in the hospital, they were not as prepared for preemie infants as they had been in the NICU. It took them awhile to find the right-sized tube. Around 12:30 p.m., she finally got to eat. The little sweetheart had gone twelve hours without food.

This was hard on her, and it was hard on me. I was there to look after my baby, and in situations like this one, I felt so helpless. She was clearly upset because of the lack of food in her tummy. I attributed the bleeding issues to her heart rate and blood pressure rising. Maybe she was even making a chewing motion with her mouth, which might have caused the bleeding.

After everything settled down, Karina got her first round of chemo, and Bill and I had our CPR class. About 8:45 p.m., Bill and Anna headed for home.

On the home front that same day, some ladies from our church went to our house to get it spic-and-span clean for Karina's homecoming. They vacuumed, dusted, scrubbed floors, and washed windows and curtains. Because the trach and the chemo had their own sets of issues, we wanted everything clean for her safety. They mostly focused on the room that Karina would be sleeping in but also attended to other areas of the house.

Even though she had the major bleed, the plan was still for us to proceed with going home. Karina also had to pass her own tests. One was a car-seat test to make sure that she could sit in her car seat for the designated amount of time without having trouble breathing.

Excerpt from CarePages

August 23, 2007

Hello Everyone,

We are still working on clarifying the time table for getting home. The docs finally came and talked realistically with us today. It looks like it might be Monday. There is still much that Bill and I have to learn (mostly Bill, but don't tell him that I said that), and we have to wait until our truckload of home health-care supplies arrives at our house. Karina needs a lot of supplies: trach-care items, feeding-tube supplies, IV supplies, pumps, emergency oxygen, suction machines (one portable, one stationary), gloves, sterile water, IV fluids, masks, alcohol wipes, etc.

I do not know about where you live, but here, the storms were awful tonight. On my way home (that's what I call it) in the shuttle, I passed about ten trees that were down on the street between the hospital and RMH. None of them was lying across the street. They were all on top of cars that were parked at the curb. One of the ladies in the shuttle said that while she was at the hospital, she heard what sounded like a train.

Before Bill comes in the morning for our marathon of training and caring for Karina on our own, she is scheduled for another CT scan. Hopefully, they will do this one in a more timely manner, instead of waiting until she has gone ten-plus hours without food. Karina had a small amount of bleeding today, but otherwise, she had a great day, sleeping through most of the daylight hours. I told her, "Karina, just sleep for the next couple of months, and then, it will all be over."

Thank you for showing your care for us through your thoughts and prayers. Please continue to pray for Karina's little body. So far, the only symptom that I have noticed from the chemo is her little red bottom.

Love in Christ,
Christie, Bill, Britta, Armin, Anna, Eva, Elaina, Greta, Jena, and Karina

P.S. I also wanted to add that when you see a picture of Karina's mouth open, you see the tumor. That is not her tongue in the pictures. Her tongue is cute, little, and pink. One friend asked if the tumor looks like a baseball in her mouth. I said, "No, it looks like a brain."

PPS Karina is six weeks old today, and she weighs over six and a half pounds.

 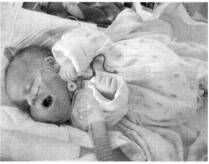

Bill came as planned the next morning, and we had our crash course in caring for our baby. We took turns sleeping in the comfortable chair. The uncomfortable chair was for the person who was on duty. When it was a person's turn, that individual had to feed her, give her medications, suction her trach, flush her IV, hold her, change her, check her vitals, and reposition her. Three hours later, the one on duty had to start the routine all over again. We passed our test and finally became legally able to care for our eighth baby. Karina also passed her car-seat test. She will be able to travel safely to our home, as soon as we receive the go-ahead.

As unbelievable as it sounds, even though chemo had only started the day before, the tumor was already starting to shrink! At this point, the plan was to go back to Children's Memorial every Friday for her chemo. I was not able to drive with her alone, as I needed to be by her side in case of trach issues. She would often get raspy, and I would have to suction her quickly. I also needed one or two adults to stay home with the other seven children, as I would be gone about six-to-nine hours, depending on traffic and how long her appointments lasted.

I had to do more scheduling. Up to that point, friends and family members had been taking turns caring for the kids since July 12 (actually before July 12 because I had quite a few Chicago appointments leading up to the delivery). We also had grandmas getting groceries and taking kids to appointments as needed. I had to keep track of everything with a little flip phone, from ninety miles away in Chicago.

One time, a friend asked to take our four oldest children for the day. I told her that the kids had to stay together. The little ones needed the stability of the bigger ones being there. Because I was gone and Bill was working, I wanted something consistent for the youngest ones, that they could count on. We had friends take them to parks and forest preserves. Two young ladies from church even took them to the county fair. It was a huge step for me to allow someone else to take our children to a busy public place such as the fair and trust that they would keep track of everyone. I knew from experience how hard that was. It was a memorable summer for the kids and a big step for my trust in God.

During my stay in Chicago, I had many visitors. Friends and family would come and spend a few hours with me, and sometimes, they would come for the whole day. I remember one day when four friends from church came. We walked to a nearby restaurant for lunch and then went shopping at a thrift store down the street. It was so nice to do something normal for a change and to have a distraction from my new routine. I enjoyed sharing laughter and tears with my friends. We made some great memories that day.

People would send gifts to Karina, some whom we had just met and didn't even know. They would send homemade blankets and afghans to her, gift cards for our family to buy gas with, and various other items that would bless us. We praise the Lord for all those people who He used to help us through our difficult summer.

12

"TODAY WE HAVE GREAT NEWS. Karina's mouth closed! Praise the Lord!" I wrote in CarePages the next day. This was huge news for us. Her mouth had been held open, even before her birth, by that huge tumor. It was so wonderful to see it close.

I checked out of RMH and spent the night in the hospital, as it was nearing the departure day. Karina's full-body CT scan had come back clean, and Karina's emergency equipment had started to arrive at the hospital. All of the portable machines that I would need to go with us wherever we went had to arrive at the hospital before we could leave. Karina also had a hearing test, which she failed because of her left ear. Not knowing if the test failure was tumor related, we would have to have it checked again during another hospital stay in the future.

I let my friends and family members who went on CarePages know that I would continue to write as time allowed. I also told them of a

Meet Karina Open House, which our church was helping us plan. We wanted people to be able to meet Karina before she had so much chemo that her immune system was depleted. I also did not want to have constant visitors at our house. Life was crazy enough with Karina's three-hour schedule and schooling the other children. I still would be having friends and family coming in to help me and to help tutor the children, as caring for Karina was a full-time job by itself.

On August 27, 2007, we finally went home from the hospital. Bill brought Eva (age seven) with him to the hospital to bring us home. They came in and helped to take the loads of equipment out, using a little wagon.

It was so surreal to actually have Karina with us in the van and be traveling home. Thoughts went whizzing through my mind: *How can I do this? Will I make it through each day? Will I be able to handle the medical emergencies? What about future bleeding issues? Will I be able to make the time to school the other kids and spend time with them? Will I ever leave the house again?*

We finally arrived home around 3:00 p.m. and found our very enthusiastic children. They were all waiting by the front door to welcome us home. The kids had waited a long time to have their mommy and baby sister come home to stay.

When we got home from the hospital, Eva and Jena's things had to be moved to a downstairs bedroom so that Karina could have the large bedroom upstairs for all her equipment. Jena did not seem to mind too much that her crib now belonged to another baby.

We also left a twin-size bed in Karina's room, as I felt I would need to sleep in there for the entire time that she had a trach. I did not think that I would be able to hear her monitor from across the hall, in my room.

Karina's new room was full. It had a crib on one wall. There was a desk along another wall that had my computer and pump, and also a dresser that held the monitors, humidifiers, and suction machines. Along the third wall, there was a closet and the changing table (loaded with chemo proof gloves, hand sanitizer, and gentle baby wipes. My bed was along the fourth wall.

Neither of us slept well the first night, and even after that, Karina would have good nights and bad nights. In order to keep her weight up, I had to keep her on the same three-hour routine day and night, which kept me from sleeping much.

Even though I was extremely busy, it was good to be home. Each night, I actually looked forward to going to bed, as each day was so exhausting (physically and emotionally) for me. After getting Karina settled down for bed, I would set my alarm for every three hours. During those feedings, I would give her formula through her feeding tube, suction the trach, and change her diaper (while wearing my special heavy-duty chemo gloves, as her chemo was not only irritating to her small, tender bottom but also to our hands if there was any skin contact). Then if she happened to be awake, I would get her settled back down, and we would both go back to sleep until the next three-hour alarm went off.

13

"CHRISTIE? DOCTOR? ANYONE? COME QUICK. She's bleeding!" Grandma Coco ran frantically out of the hospital room and looked both ways. Karina was once again bleeding profusely from her mouth, and Grandma did not know what to do to help her. I had just stepped out of the exam room for a moment, and when I came back, I saw the same kind of bleeding that she had had a few weeks earlier when I had thought she was going to bleed to death! I ran back out of the room to find someone to help. Within seconds, a nurse and an oncology doctor came back with me and stopped the bleeding.

Grandma, Karina, and I had gotten up early to leave the house by 5:30 a.m. We were supposed to be at the chemo clinic by 8:30. It was another hurry-up-and-wait day. After we arrived, we waited about half an hour. Then Karina was weighed and measured, and her blood pressure and temperature were taken. Then we waited another half hour for the doctor to check her. Then it was another half hour before the nurse came and checked her blood.

At that point, the PICC line was not allowing blood to flow out, so the nurse tried again and then went to get advice. The oncology nurse then had to order a medication to put into Karina's IV so that the blood would not clot, and she could then take the blood that she needed.

After another long wait for the medication, it was finally put into the line, and we had to let it sit for a while. When the nurse went to consult the doctors again, I decided it was a good time for me to use the bathroom. That was when the bleed occurred.

After we found someone to help us and they stopped the bleeding, we were told that we should go home. A visiting nurse would come to our house the following day to take blood through the PICC line. If that was unsuccessful, Karina would need to be admitted to the hospital to get a new PICC line and her chemo treatment.

After five long hours at the hospital, they sent us back home with nothing to show for it. Although it was disappointing, I purposefully looked for the positives in it. Karina had done great the whole day and slept on the way there and on the way home. I was also very thankful that we had been at the hospital when her mouth started to bleed, and not at home. We prayed and asked for prayer that the PICC line would work. Then we had to just wait and see what God would do. I also prayed that she would not have another bleed like that, especially while at home. I was not exactly sure what I would do if it happened again.

The home health nurse came the next day, and unfortunately, the PICC line still did not work, so I called the hospital to find out the new plan.

Excerpt from CarePages

September 5, 2007

Good Morning,

I think I know what is going on this week. On Friday morning, Karina will have surgery to put in a central line instead of the PICC line, which they are removing. The PICC line is an IV in her arm. The central line will be in her chest and lead directly to her heart. There seem to be fewer problems with central lines, and it should last through the rest of her chemo. She will also get her chemo on Friday. We should be home with her that night or on Saturday.

I asked to see her speech therapist from the NICU. We might be able to start to give her milk with a bottle while we are there, as her mouth has so much more room now, and she really likes to suck on her pacifier. As Karina doesn't need to be awake to eat, she slept all night last night and that was great for both of us, because on the three prior nights she hardly slept at all. I'm not concerned about her having her days and nights mixed up. My concern is that Karina appeared to be in pain those nights that she was awake.

Thank you for your prayers. The tumor is disappearing so quickly, even though she has only had one chemo treatment. Please keep her in your prayers as she has surgery and her next chemo dose on Friday. Also, please pray that we can find nurses in Rockford who can give her chemo so that we don't have to go into Chicago every week.

Love in Christ,
Christie for the Geaschels

CHAPTER

14

"KARINA'S JAWBONE, WHICH WAS EGGSHELL thin, has started to form and grow. Her lungs look great. The tumor continues to shrink. She went through surgery great" I wrote on CarePages Sept 7, 2007.

We had gotten home from a long day in Chicago. Karina had her central line put in, her PICC line taken out, her trach changed, and a bronchoscope of her lungs. The ENT looked at and felt the tumor. I loved it when they were efficient and got a lot done in one visit. Even though it had been a long day, it was so great to come home and report all the praises and the answered prayers that had occurred.

During the next week, Karina met her pediatrician in Rockford for the first time. She weighed in at eight pounds one ounce. To us, she had grown so much, but she was still wearing newborn-sized clothes.

Most nights she slept well and she was finally able to start moving her neck on her own. We had received a musical aquarium to hang on her crib. We purposely put it on the right side of the crib so that she would have to turn her head if she wanted to see it. It was so exciting to watch her turn her head those first few times, so that she could watch the little plastic fish swim across the ocean screen as various songs played. Each milestone for Karina was huge, and I joyfully documented them, knowing that that is unusual for the eighth child.

15

"SHE DID GREAT! THERE WAS not a sputter, a choke, or a cough" I wrote on CarePages, September 15, 2007.

We had arrived that morning in Chicago at 8:30 and met with the speech therapist for a suck study. The therapist put blue food coloring into a bottle of milk so that she could easily see if the milk went into the trach. She suctioned out the trach after Karina was done drinking, and it was clear, so Karina got permission to take one ounce by mouth a few times a day.

After the meeting with the speech therapist, we went to the oncology's day-hospital clinic for Karina's chemo. We waited about seven hours. I came to realize that the best way to stay positive about waiting was to remind myself that I got to spend the whole day with Bill. Our days at home were very busy, and with me having to sleep in Karina's room, the best time to talk was on our trips to Chicago.

Karina still had not experienced any stomach upset, and her blood counts remained good. One of the nurses told us that even though everyone else had thought that we needed to have night nurses come to our home, she had been confident all along that we could handle Karina's care on our own.

A friend emailed a hymn to me called "Day by Day."

First Verse

> *Day by day and with each passing moment, strength I find to meet my trials here. Trusting in my Father's wise bestowment, I've no cause for worry or for fear. He whose heart is kind beyond all measure gives unto each day what He deems best, lovingly it's part of pain and pleasure, mingling toil with peace and rest.*

Second Verse

> *Every day the Lord Himself is near me with a special mercy for each hour. All my cares He fain would bear*

and cheer me, He whose name is Counselor and Power. The protection of His child and treasure is a charge that on Himself He laid; as thy days, thy strength shall be in measure, this the pledge to me He made.

Third verse

Help me then, in every tribulation so to trust Your promises, O Lord, that I lose not faith's sweet consolation offered me within Your Holy Word. Help me then when toil and trouble meeting, e'er to take as from a Father's hand, one by one the days, the moments fleeting, till I reach the Promised Land. (Berg 1990, 367)

These words really spoke to me of God choosing the things that He would give to us each day. The words, "Mingling toil with peace and rest," meant that He not only knew what we were going through but also controlled and planned it for us so that we could be drawn closer to Him and become more like His Son each day.

Day by day, the tumor continued to shrink. At one point, it looked like a cave, with parts hanging down and sticking up. But as it started to shrink more, those parts were gone, and we actually had to look far to the left side of her mouth to find the tumor. The doctors felt that as the tumor shrank and became more manageable, they would surgically remove it. No one was quite sure when that would happen, but as the tumor shrunk, the thought, *When will her surgery be?* was always in the back of my mind.

Excerpt from CarePages

September 26, 2007

Hi everyone,

We had our first nonmedical, nonchurch outing today. We went to the grocery store and we went to the chiropractor.

It sure felt good to get an adjustment on my neck. My mom had to drive the van, so I could be near Karina to suction her trach. We took all seven girls with us. It was so good to get out and do something normal, and Karina slept through the whole adventure. I hadn't been to Woodman's to get groceries since the beginning of July. When we got home, Karina pulled out her feeding tube. I got her next feeding in her without putting it back in, and I am hoping that we can leave it out for a while. She took over two ounces from the bottle at that feeding. I'm not sure if she will be awake enough to take a bottle in the middle of the night, but I think that I will try it. I have attempted to nurse her a couple of times, but I might need some help. It could be difficult for her to start nursing after only taking a bottle.

We plan to get her fourth chemo treatment at our home tomorrow, as well as her blood test. She is also being evaluated for physical therapy, but I don't think she needs it.

Thank you for holding our family up in your prayers. Karina is still doing great, and she is just as healthy as ever.

Love in Christ,
Christie, Bill, Britta, Armin, Anna, Eva, Elaina, Greta, Jena, and Karina Faith

I remember that first trip to the grocery store to buy my own groceries for the family. Wow! It had been so long. I took out my checkbook, which hadn't seen the inside of a store in weeks, and I started to write July on the date's line. It took quite some time for my mind to realize that summer was over. It was now the middle of September. Time had not stood still while I was away.

16

"PLEASE PRAY TONIGHT AS WE are still working out all the details of another last-minute trip", I pleaded on CarePages, September 27, 2007.

It was the very next day, and Karina needed her feeding tube put back in. She took too long to eat, and she had not taken in enough milk at her feedings. Earlier in the morning, she was evaluated by a physical therapist, and the home-health nurse also came to check her blood.

We didn't get the call until that evening that her hemoglobin was too low and that she had to go in for a transfusion the next morning. With me not being able to drive her anywhere and the other kids too young to care for themselves, this kind of situation was always inconvenient.

Who do I call on this time? Grandparents? Friends? Should Bill miss another day of work? The decision was not always easy. Sometimes I would have to make five to ten calls so that I could fill all the positions for which I needed help. Sometimes, I did not even have twenty-four-hours' notice to give them.

The next day in Chicago was similar to the others: hurry up and wait. Bill's dad came and picked Karina and me up around 6:00 a.m. That was after I had gotten myself and Karina ready for the day, all her supplies loaded, and her four carry-on bags into the van. I also had to get everything ready so that the kids could be looked after and fed during the next six-to-twelve hours.

We got to the hospital around 8:30 a.m., and the transfusion was finally started around 11:45. The transfusion took about four hours, and then we were on our way home. I was thankful to have that day with Grandpa Jim, as I did not usually have a lot of time to spend talking with my father-in-law.

As Karina got older, she took out her feeding tube more and more often. One weekend, she took it out three times. During that stage in her life, I had started researching different bottles and ways to feed her. On the Internet, I searched for, "Bottles for babies with cleft palate," thinking that it might be a benefit to her. She could suck, but not strongly or for an extended amount of time, because the muscles in the left side of her mouth and cheek were not working. If we could help her suck, it could be much more efficient.

Karina's room was quite a sight. There was an area of her crib where all her emergency tools hung (extra trach, tape, suction catheters, and scissors). Her supply bag, which was for emergencies that happened away from home, was stored under the bed. There was also a suction machine and emergency oxygen under the bed, a monitor in the bed, and toys hanging all around for her to look at because she spent so much time in her crib.

Her humidity machine had a long tube that stretched from the dresser to the crib. We hooked the tube to a cuff that hung around her neck. She needed the humidity tube to be hooked up near her trach because she did not breathe through her mouth or nose. Without normal breathing, no natural humidity went into her throat or lungs.

Bill had attached a diagonal, wooden bar from the bottom of one side of her crib to the top rail of the other side, so that one of her feeding tubes could be hooked to it. The feeding tube was not long enough to reach from the side of the bed to Karina's NG tube. The bar worked out so nicely that we started hanging toys on it for Karina to try to reach. Twelve years earlier, my brother had made this crib for Britta, and it worked out perfectly for Karina. One home-health nurse realized how practical it was that she asked us if we had it made especially for her.

Another benefit of the crib was that the side folded down, so it was convenient for us and the nurses to get to her and work on what needed to be done. The wooden bars were wide, and we could easily tape emergency supplies to them. While they were out of Karina's reach, they were near enough for us to get to them quickly.

Staying in that room, which was down at the end of the hall, evoked so many different emotions during the time that I stayed with Karina. I missed my time with Bill. He spent time cuddling with me before he went across the hall to get some sleep, but it was not the same thing as sharing a room with the man I had married 13 years earlier.

Even though I was thankful for Karina's room, I also hoped and prayed that the days of sleeping in that room with Karina would one day be just a memory. I was thankful that I could stay with her and I was glad to do it, even though it meant lots of exhausting days and many sleepless nights.

CHAPTER

17

"SHE DID IT! KARINA NURSED!" I was so excited to write on CarePages the night of October 2, 2007.

I nursed her quite a few times that day, and then, I would give her a bottle. Sometimes I would still have to hook up the feeding tube, also. It was quite an ordeal to nurse her because her mouth was not midline (in the center of her face), and I still had to worry about the trach. I could not even see her mouth when she was on my left side.

As much as my heart wanted me to nurse her, my brain reluctantly added up the amount of time it took to nurse on both sides, make a bottle with formula to pour into her feeding tube so that her tummy was full, and then go and pump more milk in case she didn't get everything when she nursed. As much as I wanted this for her, I had to figure out if it was a practical thing to do during our busy days and while caring for our other children.

We went on with our daily schedules while we waited for our next visit to Chicago for Karina's chemo and the things that the visit would entail for us.

Excerpt from CarePages

October 5, 2007

We are home after going to Chicago once more. There's a lot on my mind this morning. Here is a synopsis of what happened yesterday.

- *We arrived at the hospital around 8:45 a.m.*
- *The CT scan started about 11:00 a.m.*
- *Karina had to have extra sedation for the scan, as she would not go to sleep. She had four doses; in the past, she had only needed one or two doses. Even after she was finally out, her little tongue kept moving.*
- *We waited until she woke up, fed her, and headed upstairs to oncology to be admitted (for chemo).*
- *Bill gave blood to have some on hand in case Karina needs another transfusion for chemo or surgery.*
- *At 4:00 p.m., hydration for chemo was finally started. At 6:00 p.m., chemo was started.*
- *We met the ENT resident, who showed us Karina's past and present CT scans. Wow! That was interesting. The tumor had originally grown up through the left jawbone, separated the inside from the outside, and made two thin layers of bone instead of one solid jaw. (Does that make sense?) There also was no visible bone in the left jaw joint on the original scans. Now, after five rounds of chemo, the jawbone pieces were*

together and actually much thicker than the right side. Praise God that as the tumor is shrinking the bone is growing.

- *As the jaw is developing, it is out of place and extra thick. That will be much easier to remedy than if the bone was missing. We had been advised to continue the chemo since she has been responding so well and staying so healthy. The oncology doctor plans to do two more rounds of chemo (another six weeks), and then we will talk to the ENT surgeon again.*

- *The oncologist is very pleased with Karina's progress. She is over eight and a half pounds! He told us that we can pull the feeding tube out. He also advised us to stop another one of her medications (I stopped one of the others last week on my own). She is only taking multivitamins and another medication, which she takes three days a week. I waited until we got home to pull the tube out so that I will have it in case of an emergency.*

- *At 7:00 p.m., chemo was finished. Karina started on six hours of post chemo IV hydration. We were told that we could leave after it was finished. We were eager to get home because Bill had a work commitment for the next day. As work had been slow, he wanted to use the opportunity that the Lord had provided.*

- *Bill napped the rest of the evening. I took care of Karina and tried to nap, but Karina had a very loud one-year-old roommate. I didn't want to wear earplugs as Bill had chosen to do.*

- *At 1:30 a.m., we were on the road. We made it home in record time, as we were able to actually go the speed limit and not be substantially slowed down by heavy traffic as we so often were.*

Thank you so much for your prayers. We can see God's hand at work in Karina's health, the growth of her bone, the increased faith and patience of Bill and me, and the list could go on and on.

With love,
Christie for the Geaschel family

We spent the next days at home. Many times, we almost put the feeding tube back in, and then, she would seem to drink more during the next meal. It was a hard decision, and when she quit gaining weight consistently, we reluctantly but also thankfully put the tube back in. How grateful we were that we had the option and that we could use it when it was necessary.

Around this time, Karina started sucking her thumb. It was very sweet to see her being able to calm herself down in this manner. Whenever she sucked her thumb, she also held onto one of her three favorite animal blankies. They were part small blanket and part animal. She had Baaa (a lamb), Bear (a bear), and Snoodle (a special one from the NICU). She would grab it with both of her little hands and then put her hands up to her mouth so that she could suck on her thumb.

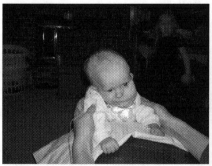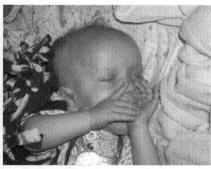

Our next concern was her left eye. I noticed that it did not close consistently and it didn't blink when something came near it. Because of these concerns, I wanted it checked by a professional.

I was continuing my ongoing bottle research. I found that Playtex nursers might be beneficial to Karina. On October 18, I went on my first outing by myself since the previous July and bought Playtex nursers. For her bottle feedings after that, I would gently squeeze the plastic bag while Karina sucked on the bottle, and she would get more milk with less effort and time. As she was now three months old, she should be able to take in more at a feeding than she had been. I just had to figure out the best way to get it into her tummy without that old NG tube. So once again, we took out the tube, hoping to keep it out permanently.

On October 26, Karina finally hit nine pounds. At three and a half months old, she was the same weight that her sister Jena had been at birth. This would also be a momentous day, as I had lined up a private physical therapist to help us, since Karina was getting further behind where a baby her age should be.

Other big news of the day was that Karina's big sister Britta had just turned twelve years old. I had trained her how to suction Karina's trach so that she could go with us to local appointments. It gave us all a little more freedom. Then we only had to find one extra adult when I had appointments. Britta was very mature for her age, being the oldest of so many siblings. Although I would not recommend most twelve-year-olds being put in a position to suction a trach or help change trach ties, I knew that she could handle it.

18

"WHEW! WHAT A DAY!" I wrote on CarePages after another long day in Chicago.

It had started the day before that, when the central line hadn't been working properly. I called Chicago to find out what to do because our home-health nurse did not have permission to use the de-clotting drug at home. The doctors in Chicago talked over some options with me and then told us to come to the hospital. That was easy for them to say.

I had to find childcare and a chauffeur for Karina and me. Britta was fine while helping on small trips around town with us, but driving into Chicago was too far for her to care for Karina. Bill couldn't leave his job that day, my mom was sick (actually ended up in the hospital herself that night), and Bills' mom couldn't leave work. I finally found some church friends who could watch the kids, and my dad was able to take time off from his electrical business so that he could chauffeur us into Chicago.

We left at 11:30 a.m. and got meds into her line around 2:45 p.m. By 4:15 the central line was finally working. We were back on the road about 5:00 and in rush-hour traffic. Just like the day I had spent with Bill's dad, I enjoyed being with my dad. It was a rare occurrence to be able to talk to him for that many hours without interruptions.

Excerpt from CarePages

November 7, 2007

Hi everyone,

I have a few things to post. On Monday, Karina started physical therapy. The PT was surprised at what Karina could do. She gave us some exercises to work on, for the areas that Karina could use help.

As we talked, the meaning of Karina's name came into the conversation. I discovered that she was a Christian too.

I also took Karina to our chiropractor this week. He worked on some tight muscles in Karina's back and adjusted her hips (pelvis), which made her legs the same length. I hadn't realized that they were off.

Today, while holding Karina in my lap, I was able to pull her up by her arms to a sitting position while she kept her head even with her body. In the past, her head would just hang there. I was so excited to see the progress that I called all the kids to come in and see.

Karina went with us to the orthodontist twice this week, as three of our girls prepared to get expanders put in. The ladies who worked there were so taken by Karina's story that they kept asking questions about her. They were very excited when she woke up to eat because they were able to see her awake.

I'll continue to keep you updated as I find time to sit at the computer.

In Christ,
Christie

On a special night in November, a friend who was a pediatric nurse came to our house. She watched all of the kids including Karina so that Bill and I could go out for the evening with another couple. That was such a blessing. I enjoyed our evening out and felt at peace, knowing Karina was OK without me there.

During the month of November, we were anticipating another CT scan to determine if we would continue chemo or if the doctors were going to opt for surgery. After weighing the pros and cons of both decisions and wondering which one would be the better outcome, I decided that instead of worrying about it or trying to decide myself, I would just trust God, Karina's Creator, with her future. I would trust the decision of the doctors. It's always a good idea to quit the fretting and worrying and leave it in the Maker's hands.

The CT scan on November 17 was uneventful. Karina did get the hiccups again, so she needed extra medication in order to get to sleep. Unfortunately, the tumor looked the same as in the last CT scan, which was frustrating. She had just gone through six more weeks of drugs being pumped into her body, with nothing to show for it. It was also surprising to hear one of the ENTs say to be prepared that when she does have surgery, they might remove her jawbone. Wow!

We talked to oncology and the surgeon. They said that they would talk together and meet with us on Monday about what the next step in Karina's care would be. In the meantime, Karina was interacting more and smiling for most people with whom she came into contact.

19

*Count it all joy, my brothers, when you face
trials of various kinds. (James 1:2 ESV)*

THIS WAS THE SCRIPTURE FROM church on Sunday. The trials with Karina's health have sure taught me a lot. They have made me much more dependent on Christ, instead of on myself and others. Ever since I was little, I have been a very dependent person. I liked to help people and liked it when they helped me.

The surgeon and the oncology doctors decided to try a new chemo drug instead of an operation. The new chemo would have new side effects associated with it. Learning problems, decreasing blood count levels, and mouth and liver sores were some of the side effects that we needed to research.

On the morning of November 27, I noticed that the inside of Karina's trach was red. I suctioned it, and there was more blood. I called the oncology doctors before 8:00 a.m., and when I didn't hear from them, I called back around 10:30. They told me to call the ENT. It was hard to focus and get anything done that day while waiting for the doctors to tell me what to do to help her.

At 1:30 p.m., I finally talked to a nurse, who told me we needed more humidity in the room. It had been a long agonizing morning of waiting. I had needed two adults to be there and ready, in case we had to rush to the hospital. Finally, the chauffeur and the babysitter were both released to go home, and I was free to start my day.

Karina had her first cold during this time, and with the coughing and sneezing (which both came through the trach in similar ways) and extra suctioning, it made sense that she needed more humidity. It just would have been nice if someone had told me that at 8:00, instead of at 1:30.

I thought back to the sermon. It was good to be reminded to be thankful in all things, not only when everything was going well.

Excerpt from CarePages

November 30, 2007

Thank you for your prayers. Karina's cold seems to be getting much better. There has been no more blood in her trach, and she is coughing and sneezing less and less.

Yesterday she was supposed to get chemo, but there was a question about dosage, so the nurse said that she would come out today. She came this morning but left again when she found out that we didn't have an emergency allergic-reaction kit at home. She called to get one ordered from our supply company, but they said that it was not one that Karina could get. We are waiting for Children's Memorial Hospital in Chicago, home health, and our supply company to get it figured out so that Karina can get her chemo this afternoon. The doctors in Chicago said that the allergic-reaction kit isn't necessary, but home health won't administer the chemo without it. So we sit and wait again.

I realized this morning the reason that I get so frustrated with pumping. A friend of mine just had twins five days ago. She called this morning, and I happened to ask her how much milk she was able to get from pumping. She gets more in one pumping session than I get in three, and I have been at it for four and a half months.

I found out that Karina's next CT scan is December 21. We might also see a plastics' specialist to find out about getting a kind of brace for Karina's head to help round it out. Her head is flat because of the way that she was positioned on her side for so many months. She could not lie on her back even if she wanted to. Her head is also misshapen as her forehead does not go straight across.

Thank you for praying for Karina and me. I know that the patience that I have can only come from Him. I have learned so much through this. It used to be that I would make plans and intend to fulfill them. Now when I plan or think to do something, I say, "If the Lord wills." I never know what the next day is going to bring. This situation has helped me to remember who is in control, and it definitely isn't me.

Have a great weekend. Remember the reason for the season. It's so easy to get distracted.

Love,
Christie

The lesson of "if the Lord wills" was also a great lesson for my other children to learn during that stage of their lives. They would often ask me, "What are we going to do tomorrow?" I would tell them the things that were scheduled. After Karina was home from the hospital, many days, I would have to go back to them and say, "Plans changed. We are going into Chicago instead." So we all quickly got to the point of saying, "The plan is," instead of making a firm statement about what was going to happen.

During the month of December, all of our children took part in two nativity programs. Biggest sister Britta was Mary, and Karina played the part of Baby Jesus. We got through both performances without having to suction the trach. Karina did great, and we did not have to worry about the baby crying loudly during the programs.

20

"IF THE TUMOR IS NOT cancerous, it will be best to leave it where it is until she is older. It will be devastating for her to lose her mandible at this age," reported the plastic surgeon. We had gone to visit him to find out more about getting a helmet for Karina's head, and he had shared this news as well.

When Karina was a newborn, I just wanted to get the surgeries over with, get rid of the trach, and let her be a normal baby. As I learned more about what she might have to go through, I thought, *Why mess with her? She can eat. She is getting therapy to learn to sit and crawl. She is so content and happy; maybe we should wait with her surgery.*

On CarePages, I asked people to pray for the doctors as they continued to figure out what to do with this rare tumor. In August, the ENT had told us, "If this tumor had formed on the calf of her leg, they would have amputated it from the knee down." That is what they were dealing with inside her mouth. We prayed fervently that God would remove the whole tumor from her jawbone and around the facial nerves. We waited for the next CT scan to find out what the plan was.

On December 21, we went into Chicago early in the morning for the scan. Karina had seemed sick during the previous few days. It turned out that she had a touch of the stomach flu, partnered with a declining hemoglobin level, which caused a decreased appetite, a sleepy disposition, and lowered oxygen levels and heart rates.

After arriving at the hospital around 8:30, Karina would not go to sleep even with sedation. After four doses, once again she got the dreaded hiccups (This was the third CT scan sedation that had given her hiccups). She then quickly proceeded into respiratory distress, which prompted me to run from the room. I could not bear to see her struggle. I could do nothing to help as the nurses worked on her. She could not cough because she was too sedated, and her oxygen levels continued to drop. The nurses scrambled to get the nebulizer treatment going. In the meantime, I regained my composure so that I could hold her while she got the treatment. Although, she was not able to get the scan done, we found out that the hiccups she had experienced in the past had been the start of respiratory distress. The CT nurses told us what sedation drugs she was not able to have anymore.

The rest of the day, Karina kept coughing a dry, hacking cough. After her oxygen levels were up, we fed her and then headed to the chemo day hospital for her chemo around 11:30 a.m. We all decided that Karina would benefit from a transfusion, which arrived at 2:30 p.m. Halfway through the four-hour transfusion, she received her chemo.

We had an opportunity to talk to her oncology doctors and the ENT. They decided to put off the surgery for an undecided amount of time; maybe as soon as two months or maybe as far away as five years. Karina was progressing so well that they did not want to put her through the deforming, debilitating surgery until she got older and stronger. Oncology would carry on with chemo until it stopped working, and they would all continue to monitor her through hospital visits and CT scans. They also told us that we could work on getting rid of the trach, which was the best news for us!

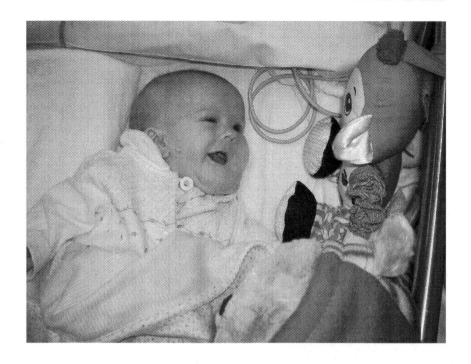

Also during this time, we were nearing the end of a six-month pop tab contest, which we had held for our family and friends. Through CarePages, we encouraged them to collect tabs from pop and soup cans. When Karina turned six months old, we would see who had the most. We would then collect, count, and donate them all to the Ronald McDonald House and give a prize to the winner. The RMH would turn them in for cash. Because of their help to me for so many weeks, I wanted to help them in return.

CHAPTER

21

"HER HEART RATE IS PERFECTLY normal for a baby her age, so why was her heart rate so high until now?" the cardiologist asked us at Rockford Memorial Hospital. We had gone in at 8:00, on the night before Christmas Eve. I had previously talked with the oncologist who was on call in Chicago and the pediatrician who was on call in Rockford, to inform them that Karina's heart rate kept dropping into a zone so low that the alarms would go off. No one seemed to be overly concerned, but since they could not explain it, they told us to go to the emergency room.

Bill and I followed orders, and arranged childcare for the children, loaded up Karina and all her portable gear, and headed to one of the hospitals in our town. We got to the ER. We were admitted and put in a room where we waited and waited. After twenty hours of chest x-rays, an EKG, a test for rotavirus, and a talk with the cardiologist, we learned that her heart rate was in a normal range but that her monitor had to be readjusted for her age so that the alarm wouldn't go off. I wondered the reason why everyone had failed to mention the tiny detail: as she grew, her heart rate would not always be in the same range, and over time it would be lower than when she was a newborn.

We made it out of the hospital just in time to celebrate Christmas with my family on Christmas Eve. Karina was perfectly fine, and her monitor was completely quiet, because the new settings had been put in place.

Excerpt from CarePages

December 30, 2007

The latest news is that Karina's tumor has shrunk enough that she can suck on her bottom lip! That might sound silly to be excited about, but knowing that she couldn't even attempt to close her mouth for the first few months of her life, this is big news! She is doing great, and now that we've adjusted her monitor, we are all back to sleeping through the night again.

Our next Chicago trip is scheduled for January 7. Karina will be fitted for her plastic helmet, which will mold her head to the right shape. Another CT scan is planned. We will soon schedule the tests that need to be done in order to dispose of the trach.

Thank you all for your support to our family. Thank you for keeping up with our CarePages, praying for us, and all the many ways that you have stood by our side these past months. We have so much to be thankful to God for. He brought us through 2007. We look forward to 2008 and what lies ahead for Karina and the rest of the family.

Love,
Bill, Christie, Britta, Armin, Anna, Eva, Elaina, Greta, Jena, and Karina Faith

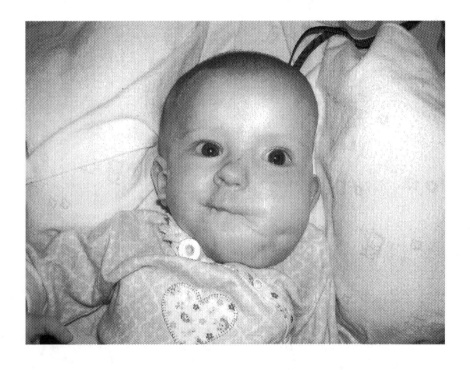

22

"BILL! I HEAR KARINA'S VOICE!" I yelled across the hall to wake up Bill. Thankfully, he woke up the first time I yelled. I had awakened moments earlier, hearing a baby's voice. That was not normal for a baby with a trach., as the device is below the vocal chords, which means air does not travel past it. She was not supposed to have a voice. It sounded like a muffled cry and a gasp.

After Bill had stumbled into the room, half asleep and half awake, he and I assessed the situation and realized that the trach was still in but probably plugged. I quickly tore open the emergency trach while Bill took out the plugged one. We made a record-breaking trach change, and then Karina started to cough. As I started suctioning, I was so relieved and thankful that she had been able to breathe even though the other one had been plugged.

I was also thankful that I still slept in her room, that I had not yet moved across the hall to Bill's and my room. I had thought about allowing Britta to move in with Karina, but I did not think a twelve-year-old would be able to wake up that fast or quickly assess an emergency situation. I again decided that I would remain with Karina until the trach was gone. The situation made us hopeful that it would not be long before the breathing tube could come out, though, because she had been able to breathe during that time that it was plugged.

On January 12 we ended our pop tab contest. We had gathered about sixty-five thousand tabs. We were so excited to be able to donate those to the Ronald McDonald House, which had helped me during those seven weeks at the beginning of Karina's life. One family brought in sixteen thousand. We had to confess that we did not count each and every tab. We counted the first three thousand and realized that they fit perfectly into a plastic Folger's Coffee can. We then used that to measure the large amounts by the three thousands. We had another container that held two hundred tabs perfectly. Anything less than that, we counted ourselves. It was a great math project for our homeschooled kids.

During January, Karina was not gaining weight very well, so we started her on some homemade pureed foods and some store-bought baby food. We also received her handicapped placard so that it would be easier for me to take the kids out on my own. I had to carry her oxygen (which is what qualified her for the placard), monitor, portable suction machine, emergency supply bag, and diaper bag with me everywhere that I went. It was much easier to go places when we were able to park close to our destinations, and we had extra room around the van for an easier entrance and exit.

I had a newfound freedom. I could take my eight kids out to the grocery store by myself, and it was wonderful. I am sure that we got a lot of stares as our little parade marched through Woodman's Market. As we proceeded along, Karina had her own stroller, which perfectly held her infant car seat, her bags, and equipment. We also usually used a cart that four children could sit in; otherwise, we brought in our double stroller and then used a cart for the groceries.

Many times over the years, our children have insisted that Woodman's Market in Rockford, Illinois, had the large carts that seated four children just because of our family. Armin was usually the one who heroically pushed the large cart while I pushed Karina. Anyone who did not fit in a cart, walked alongside it and helped in gathering our weekly purchases.

Toward the end of January, we were anticipating the possible removal of Karina's trach and getting her helmet, which would help her head become more round. The plastics' doctor was not too confident in the helmet, as Karina's head was very misshapen. He was not sure that it would even stay in place when she turned her head from side to side. There was much to wait for and anticipate.

On January 17, Karina got her helmet. As she grew, the cushions in the helmet would keep the larger areas of her head from growing, while only allowing her to grow in the areas where there was space in the helmet for it. She really did not mind it, and it looked so cute on her. The helmet was white with little pink and green flowers, and her name was on the front. She wore it for twenty-three hours a day. We could only take it off during her daily sponge bath and while the helmet was drying. She tended to get very sweaty underneath it. We realized that it was a good time of year for her to get the helmet, as it would keep her little head warm through the winter months.

Excerpt from CarePages

January 18, 2007

We're home again. After a long day, we came home with the trach still in place. Her bronchoscope was scheduled for 1:00 p.m., so we quit feeding her at 8:00 a.m. She finally went into surgery at 3:30. Her ENT was sure that we could take Karina's trach out, but he was uncertain about taking it out during a weekend, when there were not as many doctors on duty. His other reason to leave it in is in anticipation of her having another CT scan with anesthesia in a few weeks. It's much easier to give her oxygen with a trach than it is to intubate her for the scan.

She did get her two skin tags removed from her face, so that was something accomplished. Also, there is some great news. The ENT can't feel the tumor in her mouth anymore! Maybe she won't need much more chemo. I was disappointed that she didn't get her trach taken out, but I can understand his reasoning. It sounds like it won't be too much longer that she'll have it.

We also dropped off all the pop tabs at RMH. Thanks for the donations. Thanks for sticking with us.

In Christ,
Christie

On January 26, I posted to CarePages, mostly asking for prayer. Karina seemed to be having stomach problems, and the doctors did not link it to chemo. I wanted to find something different to feed her, as unfortunately, my pumping days had ended. I had also started doing research on facial paralysis, realizing that Karina's facial muscles did not work. The facial nerve also affects hearing, eye closure, balance, and all facial movement on that side. Our prayer was to find someone who could help us with her facial nerve.

We were also praying that we would soon be able to stop chemo and, of course, to get the trach out before long. We praised God for helping Karina stay so healthy, protecting her from fevers, the flu, colds, and anything else that those around her had. Lastly, I asked for prayer for patience.

We had spent many days inside, not going anywhere. On the one day that I finally decided to load up all the kids and venture out to the store, the van died, and we had to cancel our day trip. Each day seemed to be a different adventure, and I was longing for a new normal.

23

"KARINA IS GAINING WEIGHT BETTER, and she has now passed eleven pounds," I wrote in CarePages on February 2, 2008. We were so glad that she was gaining weight. It was during that time that I started giving her goat's milk. I added a dropper of her baby vitamins and an ice cube of homemade chicken-bone broth to each bottle. I had read that bone broth was beneficial in so many ways. I also did not like giving her baby formula, and felt that the goat's milk was healthier for her. After much research, I came up with my own recipe for Karina's bottles.

Karina was doing great using her helmet. She would roll from side to side and actually move around in her bed. She was much more active. She was getting closer to being able to sit by herself, and her therapist was very encouraged by her mobility. It was my opinion that once Karina learned that she could move on her own, she would be determined to try to move in different ways. There was no stopping her progress.

The plan at that point was to take the trach out on February 13, but I had learned not to get my hopes up. There were too many variables that I could not control. Some of those variables included the amount of staff at the hospital, the health of Karina, the condition of her tumor, and many other things that I might not even know about.

On February 5, we went to my cousin's house in downtown Chicago to spend the night, as we had a 6:00 a.m. appointment for a CT scan the next morning at Children's Memorial Hospital.

Excerpt from CarePages

February 6, 2008

We made it home. When we left Chicago around 10:30 a.m. to come home, it hadn't started snowing there yet. There was just lots of rain. It didn't take long before we hit the snow, though. At some points, we were the only car in sight. I asked Bill if the roads had been closed without informing us. We saw at least ten vehicles on the side of the road. Some were flipped over, and others were facing the wrong direction.

Karina did great this morning. I woke her up to feed her at 2:00 a.m. We arrived at Children's at 6:00, and they were actually on time for the CT at 7:30. At 8:15, she was already awake enough to eat, and then we moved to post-op recovery. After that, we went up to the day hospital for chemo and a dressing change, and then we were on our way. Even though it had been hard getting up so early, I'm thankful that we had the 7:30 appointment so that we could be on our way home as quickly as we did.

This snow didn't seem to be letting up. Some of the roads were already down to one lane. Karina slept the whole way home, which was another blessing. Those of you in the Rockford and Chicago area, stay home if you can.

Thanks for your prayers. I should be able to update you on the scan that they took after we go into Chicago next Wednesday. We didn't want to take the extra time to find her doctors to read the scan for us.

Love,
Christie

I was so glad that Bill had been with me in Chicago. I'm not sure that I would have made it home if I had been the one driving.

24

"THE TUMOR HAS NOT CHANGED at all since October," The oncology nurse told me over the phone. I could not believe what I had heard! The doctors, the nurses, our friends, Bill and I all thought that the tumor had continued to shrink. This was an agonizing shock. Karina's oncology nurse had just called, and she too had thought that the tumor had been disappearing. Her only explanation had been that it was because Karina was growing and the tumor was not, which made it look smaller. We were very discouraged, to say the least.

Now we needed prayer for the next decision. *Should they continue to administer chemo in case it was at least keeping the tumor from growing? Should they stop chemo and see what would happen? Should they try a different drug?* We knew that it might change things in regard to the trach, especially if they had to stop chemo to see what would happen. We asked people to pray for the doctors to have wisdom, for Bill and me to have peace, and for us to keep our focus on God and His plan for Karina's life and not on what we wanted. After that, we just had to wait to find out the next step.

On February 10, Karina ended up in the hospital with respiratory syncytial virus (RSV). She had gotten a bad cough and fever, and she had even started to become lethargic. I thought it might be pneumonia. I was praying that they wouldn't put her with other sick kids, which could have caused her to catch something else.

They did not keep her at the hospital, as they said it was a virus and that it would only last three to five days. We were already on day four at that point. They did some blood tests while we were there and told us that they would contact us if they found anything that we needed to know. I decided that I would not plan on the trach removal happening anytime soon. Because of the cough she had, I knew it would be out of the question.

Excerpt from CarePages

February 12, 2008

Well, here we are back at Children's Memorial Hospital. Yesterday, we got a call that one of the tests done on Karina on Sunday night came back showing a bacterial infection in Karina's bloodstream. A second blood test was done at our home last night to confirm the results. We were told that it might take five days to confirm. It has come back already, showing that Karina does have a bacterial infection in her blood. We have to go in for forty-eight hours of IV antibiotics. One of the biggest risks is that the bacteria can travel through her bloodstream and then possibly go to her brain.

I checked with her pediatrician about going somewhere in Rockford, but he thought it would be best if we came back to Children's Memorial Hospital. Karina and I will stay at least until Thursday and possibly longer. There is a chance that she will need to get her central line taken out and a PICC line put back in.

This morning, I called her oncologist to say that we didn't want Karina to get chemo this week. We really felt that she needed a break and to get over both the RSV and the blood infection. When I explained my case, they consented.

Please keep her in your prayers. Pray that she will get better quickly and that there won't be any complications. She is still very sick from RSV. Her heart races, her oxygen desats (drops), and she is very lethargic. She is usually only awake to eat. Then she goes right back to sleep.

In Christ,
Christie

PS At 11:30 a.m., I got a call to hurry and get to the hospital. We hurried there. Now it is 6:40 p.m., and no IVs have been started. Some additional info is that the infection is not necessarily in her blood. It is definitely in her central line, so they will treat her through the line. It might not be into her actual blood yet. This staph infection can be treated with antibiotics.

Since they haven't yet started, I don't see us getting home until Friday, but I am always open to surprises. She was put on oxygen. I think they finally believe me when I say that she keeps desating.

I'll keep in touch since I have the computer and not much else to do. I did bring some books, so I'll try to read those.

Christie

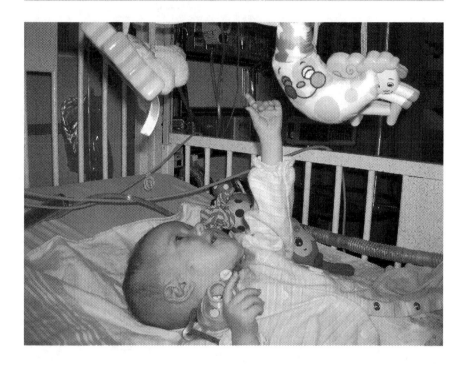

We stayed at the hospital through the next day. I had my own issues to deal with, as I had left home without money, and I did not own a debit card at that time. When Karina was living at Children's Memorial, and I stayed at the RMH, I was used to getting coupons for free food from the hospital (because of the fact that I was pumping my milk for Karina). When the nurses realized that I had not eaten since arriving the day before, they gave me three boxes of Cheerios, three cartons of milk, and three cartons of juice. They also got me some coupons for free food to use in the cafeteria. I was so thankful that they cared and helped me.

Every few hours the nurses would come in and take some of Karina's blood to the lab to see if the infection was gone. They would also give her one to two hours of IV antibiotics every four hours. Karina was in isolation because of the RSV, and I had to wear a gown and mask (I really struggled with claustrophobia while trying to sleep with a mask on). I got permission to take off the gloves as long as I promised to wash my hands well every time I left the room.

At one point, we were told we could go home the next day, but then the nurse remembered that Karina was still on oxygen. She could not go home if her oxygen would go under 90 percent while awake or 88 percent while sleeping.

While I was at the hospital, I was thankful to see some of Karina's nurses, doctors, and therapists who we had not seen since August. They were all encouraged by how well she was doing.

On February 14, we were given the go-ahead to go home. They sent us home with oxygen, which we could use as needed, and they changed her antibiotic so that we only needed to give it to her once a day. The oncologists also told us that Bill and I needed to make the decision of whether we would continue Karina's chemo. Wow! That was a hard decision. We really needed prayer for that one. We were both surprised that it was up to us and was not a decision that they were going to make.

After much prayer and weighing the pros and cons, we decided to continue chemo, at least until the trach was out. The oxygen that we took home was only used one night, and then Karina did much better after that. The infection in the central line seemed to come and go. It was very confusing to us all.

I was so glad to get back home because all my kids were getting the same cough that Karina had, and I wanted to be able to care for them too. A week after the kids got over the RSV, they all started coming down with another virus. I kept Karina in her room, and I wore a mask, trying to keep her from getting it. I knew that she would end up back in the hospital if she got a fever. Our other children had temperatures of 105 degrees, coughs, and sore throats, but thankfully, Karina didn't get it! Praise God!

25

"WELL SHE DID IT! KARINA is without her trach!" I was so excited to type these words on CarePages, on the night of March 4, 2008. I was unsure of what to expect when we went into the hospital that day. I remember being concerned for her, because she had never breathed through her mouth or nose. I wondered what she would think about the whole situation. I thought that at her age, she might be fearful to do something so new. I was wondering if she would succeed, or if we might possibly be going back home with the trach.

In the morning, the ENT came into the little room where we were waiting. The first step was to put in a solid metal trach, which was called a plug. Of course, Karina could not breathe through it but could slightly breathe around it. We were uncertain for the first hour or so because she would become frustrated and spend a lot of time coughing and crying. Because it was scary to watch, I was close to tears observing her struggle to breathe with her mouth. She had so much trouble the first few minutes that the trach was covered, I was sure they were going to send us back home with her trach.

After those very uncertain minutes, which seemed like hours, she did great! Her noises did not surprise her as much as I thought they would, but she certainly enjoyed making them.

After the ENT nurse felt that Karina was stable, they admitted her to her own room. During the time that we were at the hospital, she took her bottles, slept, laughed, cried, and even made cooing noises. Oh, it was so great to hear her voice! I loved to hear her happy sounds, and I also loved to finally hear her cries.

The next day, they planned to take the solid, metal trach out and to remove the trach ties (which held the trach in place on her neck). The solid trach was left in overnight so that the hole would not start to close up and jeopardize their chances of putting in the trach again if needed. They would put a Band-Aid over the trach hole. They would then watch her for another twenty-four hours. After another couple of days, we would no longer need to carry the emergency bag that we had carried for the past six months. After two days without her trach, it could not have been replaced without surgery. Wow, this was going to make such a difference. We would have so much freedom.

Excerpt from CarePages

March 6, 2008

We are home without the trach! She did well over the past two days, and we arrived home around noon today.

While at Children's, we (Karina and I) visited some of the NICU nurses who took care of her during her first six and a half weeks of life. They were so encouraged to see her and that she was doing well. I thanked them for giving me nurses' training so that I could care for Karina 24-7 at home. They were surprised that we had gone home without a live-in nurse.

We also saw the neonatologist who was at her delivery and her physical therapist from her early days. During her stay, we also talked to her oncologists and decided that we wanted to quit chemo and to see what would happen. She is to go back in a couple of months for a CT scan.

Until then, we only have to change her central line dressing once a week. I will continue to flush her line daily. There will be no more suctioning, antibiotics, chemo, blood tests, Mommy having to room with her, etc. I also realized that there would be no more sitting through church service because I now had a baby who could make noise.

Thank you so much for your prayers. This was a big week for Karina and the rest of the family. We are so thankful to get over this major hurdle.

Love,
Christie

Getting rid of the trach brought even more blessings than we anticipated. Karina was able to be on her tummy more, and she was getting stronger and stronger. She also started playing with her toes for the first time.

Within a few days, we got rid of the trach humidifier, monitor, and emergency oxygen. It was surreal giving them up, as those things had been part of her life since her birth. It was like taking care of an entirely different baby. We could go places whenever we wanted to. I did not have to sleep in her room anymore. I did not have to be close by while she napped because without the trach, I would hear her cry when she awakened. I also did not have to depend on monitors to let me know when she was awake, sad, hungry, or lacking in oxygen.

26

"THE MAIN THING IS TO remember what has to remain sterile and what does not need to be sterile," the home health nurse told me. Thus I had just passed another nursing test, and I was legally able to change Karina's central line dressing on my own. I could not take all the credit though, as Britta had to be by my side and hold Karina's hands away from what I was doing.

Just imagine me right by Karina's face, holding all those fascinating things right in front of her. She could not touch any of them; otherwise, they would become contaminated. Britta had the job of holding her wiggly, squirming arms while I was tested on my ability to perform the dressing change, which I had seen done countless times over the past months. We were able to take one more step of independence as a family, as the home-health nurse, who had come at least once a week since we had come home from the hospital, was eliminated from our weekly routine.

Another big change in our lives was the addition of speech therapy for Karina. At the first appointment, the speech therapist was very encouraged by how well Karina was doing, in spite of the fact that she had had a trach for seven and a half months. The other factors that were against her were her mild-to-severe hearing loss, a deformed mouth and jaw, and a tongue that had not been able to move for months. The therapist commented positively on Karina's volume, the noises that she had already learned to vocalize, her eye contact, and the fact that she cried when she wanted something.

Looking back, I think that it really helped that I was by her side from the beginning, responding to her emotions even though she could not be heard. I know how busy nurses get, and in the hospital, they would not normally have time to sit there and watch her heart rate to know when she needed something. Instead, they would have changed her, fed her, and taken care of her needs at the three-hour scheduled times. If I had not been there, she might not have known to cry for her wants. That was when I understood the therapist's amazement at Karina's crying for something so soon after getting the trach out.

We continued to be amazed and thankful to God for every step that He brought us through. We were also very thankful for our little blessing, Karina Faith.

Karina finished wearing the helmet on March 31. It was good to see the before and after scans. The plastics' surgeon wanted to see her every few months, but he did not plan to do any kind of surgery in the near future.

She had another hearing test; the results were still not definitive. Together, her ears could hear, but audiologists could not test them separately yet.

She continued to grow and get stronger as the chemo left her system.

Excerpt from CarePages

April 5, 2008

I just had to share this little update. I got a call from Karina's supply company. They said that there had been a large recall on heparin (the solution I had put into her central line daily to keep it from clotting). They told me to check my boxes and give them the lot numbers. As it turns out, the box that we had just finished the night before had been safe to use, but the one that we were going to start had been recalled. I was so thankful that I hadn't flushed her line that morning, which would have been one of the recalled heparin boxes. God is so good.

We went to a farm today, and Karina hung out in her baby carrier that I was wearing. She was thrilled when she saw the horses, baby goats, dogs, cats, and her siblings running around. She just sat there kicking her feet and getting excited.

Here is an update on Karina's feedings. Karina has gained about half a pound a week since getting off chemo. She is around fourteen pounds now. She eats either a whole jar of baby food or an entire mashed banana at each meal. She also eats graham cracker sticks, fresh pumpkin bread, and Cheerio-like cereal. Tonight, she had mashed carrots. She also loves yogurt.

She is getting so much stronger. She can bear weight on her legs for quite a while now. She is also sitting for longer amounts of time and stabilizing herself when she leans too far one way or the other.

In Christ,
Christie

We hadn't realized how much the chemo had been affecting Karina's weight gain. She changed so drastically during those next few weeks. Once she learned that she could control her body and voice, she improved and progressed quickly.

27

"DA-DA-DA-DA-DA-DA-DA NA-NA-NA-NA," KARINA SAID AS her first non-vowel sounds. She was nine and a half months old, and she was finally starting to babble. It sure did not appear that her deformed jaw and the remnant of tumor were going to slow her down much longer.

She had passed her hearing test a week or two earlier. We were told that she could hear well enough to learn to speak and to respond to what was spoken to her, and that was good enough for us at this age, even though we didn't know how affected the left ear was. She started to respond to our words by waving when we said, "Bye-bye." She also tensed her arm muscles and made fists when we asked where her muscles were.

Karina loved to eat avocados, squash, eggs, bread, pasta, carrots, bananas, broccoli, tuna, salmon, applesauce, and more. She would eat everything that was appropriate for her to eat without teeth. She now weighed about sixteen pounds.

She loved to be outside. At any opportunity, we would go outdoors. Forest preserves, walks around the neighborhood, bike rides, and picnics were some of our favorite spring activities to do with the family.

We held a fundraising garage sale to help us with Karina's medical expenses. Lots of friends and family members donated to the sales. They donated clothing, household items, quilts, toys, and many other things. We held the sales in three different neighborhoods, on three different weekends, and we had wonderful results. We had the first sale at our house, and then we moved what was left over to our friends' houses to get more customers in different areas of town. When people asked what the fundraiser was for, we enjoyed telling people about Karina and her story. We also put up fliers, which had photos and a brief description as to why we needed the funds.

Excerpt from CarePages

May 7, 2008

We're home again. Karina did great today during her CT scan. This was our best trip ever. As she got older, I wasn't sure if it would get easier or harder to go for so many hours without food. Today showed us that it was much easier than past scans were.

This morning at 6:30, she got some milk, which a friend had graciously pumped for her. Throughout the morning, she was happy and mostly content. Her scan started around noon. By 1:00, she was awake and ready to try some liquid. She had her first bottle of juice. She downed it like she'd been drinking juice forever. She slept the whole way home, and by the time we arrived, she was ready for some goat's milk and real food.

We saw many of her previous doctors and nurses today, and everyone was pleased with how she had been growing and learning. We brought her in to see her NICU nurses also.

Her oncologist called this evening. He told us that he had had a quick meeting with radiology and that from first observation, the tumor looked to be the same size, even though we had stopped the chemo. This is great news, as we have been praying that it would not grow back.

They could not take her central line out as we had hoped, but maybe within the next month we can have it removed. When we go in for that procedure, we also plan to get her trach hole stitched closed, as it is still partly open. When she blows through it, it sounds like a cell phone on vibrate mode. Once we get her central line out, and her trach hole stitched up, she can finally take a real bath. Until then, she will still get sponge baths, as there is too much danger of getting the central line wet or water into her lungs through the trach hole. That's about it.

In Christ,
Christie for the Geaschel family

28

"KARINA IS GETTING HER FIRST tooth!" I excitedly wrote on CarePages. On May 15, 2008, at 10 months old, she cut her first tooth with no signs of there being a tooth coming in. We knew the teeth were there because we saw them in the CT scans, but with chemo side effects, we didn't know how late they would show themselves. Karina also started getting on her hands and knees and rocking, forward and backward.

Excerpt from CarePages

May 15, 2008

We praise God daily for how well Karina is doing. Our little miracle baby has had no chemo side effects, and no problems eating, hearing, or communicating, in spite of the fact that she had a trach for seven and a half months and she was born with a tumor and deformed jaw. She got rid of the trach on the first try, even though she didn't know life without it, and the list goes on and on. Thank you for your continued prayers for Karina.

Love, Christie

Two weeks later, Karina was starting to crawl forward, and she could easily turn from her back to her stomach. She loved to play on the floor, and she would move all over and in many directions.

As she got older, her central line was harder to care for. It took three of us to do the dressing changes: one to change the dressing, one to hold both of her hands and keep her mind occupied, and one to hold up a blanket so that she wouldn't breathe on the line and contaminate it. When she had the trach, there hadn't been the same issues with her breath as there was now. We were eagerly anticipating the removal of the central line, because we had to constantly watch that she wouldn't pull it out. It was such a tempting "toy" and easily within reach. One day while I was changing her clothes, she had discovered that it was there.

Toward the end of May, Karina came down with a high fever. Thankfully, she ended up getting blood taken at Rockford Memorial Hospital, and we did not have to go all the way to Children's Memorial. When the fever spiked a few nights in a row, we realized that other kids at church had the same virus. We quit worrying that it might be another blood infection and just waited to see what would happen.

Excerpt from CarePages

June 15, 2008

Here's what's new. Karina is now eleven months old. Her surgery is scheduled for Friday morning. The plan is for Bill, Karina, and me to go into Chicago on Thursday night and stay at my cousin's house so that we will be much closer to Children's for our 7:00 a.m. arrival. Her surgeries will last one and a half hours, which doesn't sound long, as long as it's not your child. They will stitch up her trach hole, as well as fix it cosmetically. Then the oncologist will take out her central line. We plan to go home Saturday morning.

Some things will be different this time:

1. *She is older and moves around more. She doesn't just lie there on her back looking at a mobile above her.*
2. *She is used to being out of bed and playing on the floor.*
3. *She is more in tune with what is going on. Nurses waking her up at all hours to check her vitals will really be annoying.*
4. *She will have an IV, which she hasn't had since August when she got the PICC line put in.*

I know that all is in the Lord's hands. It's just never pleasant to see anyone that you love go through surgery, no matter how small the procedure is.

Another prayer request is for her vocal sounds. She does da-da and na-na sounds, but we haven't heard ba, ma, or pa sounds, which developmentally should be next. At this point, I'm not sure if her mouth can close enough.

In Christ,
Christie for the family

On June 20, she had her surgeries. They were done by 2:30 p.m. She did better than we had expected her to. While at Children's we met a new oncologist, who had been studying Karina's case since December. He really felt that her tumor was a *hemangioendothelioma* and that it would continue shrinking on its own. He sounded very optimistic that she might not need a surgery to remove the rest of the tumor but that she might only need some reconstruction in the future.

Surprisingly, we got to the hospital earlier in the morning than needed, so we visited the NICU nurses, the neonatologist who had been at Karina's delivery, and her oncology nurse. We always enjoyed seeing her past doctors and thanking them for their part in her care. We would also try to give brief updates of the new things that were happening.

Excerpt from CarePages

June 25, 2008

I didn't plan to post an update so soon, but there is lots of recent news. First, Karina has healed wonderfully from the surgeries. She and I are enjoying our new freedom with no central line and no blowhole in her neck. She had her first bath on Monday and we were encouraged by how well she adjusted. She was splashing with her feet, and she enjoyed playing with the water that was dripping off the washcloth.

On Tuesday, she had her checkup with the plastics' surgeon in Glendale. Both he and his nurse thought that she looked great. They were surprised at how much she had changed since March. The helmet nurse asked if she could share Karina's story when she gave lectures in the fall and spring. She said that when kids had disabilities that were as severe as Karina's, they didn't usually wear a helmet.

I found out that most of the doctors advised our plastics' surgeon against making a helmet for Karina. They thought that if her tumor was malignant, the shape of her head wasn't going to matter. I was also surprised that they really allowed her to wear the helmet for my sake because it was something that "mom could do to help her," when my hands were so tied from doing anything else. After seeing her progress and finding out that the oncologist really felt that this tumor was going to go away on its own, they realized that they made the right decision in helping her in this "one little area".

As my mom and I were talking and praising God on the way to the appointment, I realized even more the wisdom that God had given the ENT surgeon regarding his decision to cancel her surgery back in August (removing the tumor, her jaw, and all connecting nerves). Knowing now that the tumor will shrink, it would have been devastating if she had gone through the surgery when it wasn't necessary. God's miracles come in many shapes and sizes. Although it was hard at the time to make that last minute change, we were learning to trust God that His heart is for us.

Today Karina shocked us all. I had put her to bed, and I was in the process of putting some of her sisters down for the night, when I happened to peek into her room. She was standing in her crib! She fell down and did it three more times. It's hard to believe that four months ago, she couldn't make noise, couldn't roll over, had hardly even been on her tummy, and didn't have much arm or leg strength. It probably helps that she is still under seventeen pounds, and she can pull herself up easily.

Karina got sunglasses today. I have been thinking about the effects of sun and wind on her left eye, as it still doesn't always close and I've been wondering what to do about it. All winter and spring, she was in the infant car seat with a blanket draped over the top. Now she wants to be

*part of what is going on, so I can't keep doing that. Her
grandparents went to Walmart and picked up a couple of
infant-sized pairs. They can be secured by Velcro in the
back, and I think she will learn to like them.*

Love,
Christie for the Geaschels

Another new thing that she could finally do was drink from a cup.
With her mouth being off-center and muscles being weak on the left
side, it was hard for her to hold her cup and drink. To practice, I would
put her in the tub, and while bathing her, I would give her a cup of clean
water and have her practice drinking. The water would stream down her
tummy, but a little bit would get into her mouth.

Without the normal feeling on the left side of her mouth, she never
knew if she was drooling. We had to use large rubber bibs when she was
in her high chair; otherwise, much of her food would end up in her lap.
I used the bibs with the wide-open pockets. After her meal, she would
finish another whole course out of the pocket of her bib.

29

"SHE GOT TO TOUCH A toad, play in the sand, and even put her feet into the water a couple of times," I reported on CarePages after we had returned from Karina's first trip to the family cabin. She had also turned a year old. She was definitely a true one-year-old. She was crawling all over the house, standing up, and overall, very curious. Karina had also gotten to see her first fireworks' display. She complained a bit until I assured her that it was OK. She enjoyed playing in the sand and touching the lake's water. I was so glad that we had purchased her sunglasses, as they were very beneficial in keeping the sun, sand, and water out of her eyes while she played on the beach.

She would sit on the beach in her little swimming suit, pick up handfuls of sand, and let it fall through her fingers. She liked the water and letting the waves come up on her fingers and toes. Thankfully, she was not ready to go fully into the water yet, as she probably would not have had enough respect of this newfound, cold, wet, and wavy "toy" (the water).

The other big news was that our family members were interviewed by a reporter from *Ladies' Home Journal* for the December issue. As I was interviewed over the phone, I looked back over the year of CarePages so that I could remember dates, important events, and emotions that I had gone through during the first year of her life. So much was already a blur, and it was hard to remember the details without the assistance of my own journal entries on CarePages.

At that point, we were still working on her sounds, as da-da-da-da and na-na-na-na were the only sounds that Karina would use. It was amazing that her language was our biggest prayer request when her first birthday arrived, after going through so many medical situations and emergencies for so long.

It had become obvious that Karina was not progressing with her speech. She would sit and yell for her food. We were told by the speech therapist that we had to expect more from her and to really encourage any noises that she would make. After that appointment, when Karina would yell, I would either show her a sign language sign or use a noise that I knew she could make. Then I would wait until she did it, before giving her what she wanted. It really showed us that if we did not cater to her, but we expected more from her, she would excel.

Excerpt from CarePages

August 28, 2008

We continue to be amazed by progress. Last week Karina's physical therapist said that for now, Karina is right where a baby of her age should be. As there are not any physical issues for her to work on, she suggested we use the rest of Karina's therapy sessions on speech, instead of physical therapy.

We went back to speech today, and it was so exciting to tell the therapist of the progress that we have seen since going there two weeks ago. Karina asks for food (nu-nu-nu-nu, her form of num-num). She has also started to stick out her tongue and move it around. Just recently, she made noises with it. The ba sound has become part of her vocabulary. We really tried for this one. She copies the kids when they make noises that they know she can make. Overall, she is a lot more vocal than she was two weeks ago at the last appointment. She also shakes her head for the word no; and points with her index finger when we ask where something is.

Thank you so much for your prayers. Also, in the past couple of days, she has started to close her left eye. Normally she would only do that when she was asleep but never voluntarily or even as a reflex. A few times, she has taken a couple of steps, and she has also stood without holding onto something. We will continue to update you as she progresses more and more.

In Christ,
Christie for the Geaschels

30

"I'M NOT COMFORTABLE DOING THE scan with sedation, as Karina has a past history of allergic reaction, but I don't want to have to send you back home either," the CT technician told us on September 14, 2008. This scan had already been approved by her oncology doctors. They felt that it would be OK for her to be sedated again, now that the trach was gone, she was older, and they could use medication other than the one that she was allergic to.

It was 9:30 a.m., and we had left the house at 5:30 to get to the hospital. Now we were wondering what was next. The CT technician went to get permission for an anesthesiologist to do the CT with him (which they usually only do on the first Wednesday of the month). We waited and waited, as they were in a three-hour MRI.

When they came out, the nurse came to put the IV into Karina's vein. This was the first time I would miss her central line, especially as we discovered that her veins were not very strong or healthy because of the effects of chemo. The nurses first attempts failed, and then she decided to let the anesthesia specialists try. Two men came in and again tried to put in the IV. At this point, Karina started crying every time she saw someone either wearing a blue gown or wearing a mask, because she anticipated that they were coming to try to stick more needles in her. The anesthesiologists tried to use a couple of veins, which also collapsed, and they told us that they were going to have to go to plan B (or was it plan C). They would put a mask on her to get her to sleep and then insert the IV in while she was sleeping.

Most of the time this was going on, Grandma Coco, who had come in with us for the five-minute CT scan, had to be outside of the room, as it was too distressing for her. By the time they took Karina in for the CT scan, it was 11:30. A few minutes later, the anesthesiologist came into the waiting room and said that Karina was asleep with the IV in her foot. Forty-five minutes later, we were able to see her in recovery, where she downed three small bottles of juice (Did I mention that this was for a five-minute CT scan?).

An hour later, we were dismissed, and we went to find the oncologist. By the time we found him, he already had her records, and he was roaming the hospital looking for us as he had expected to see us a couple of hours earlier. He commented that everything looked good, the tumor had not changed, and we could wait a whole year before doing another scan. He still wanted to see her every three months, which was not nearly as hard for us as doing more CT scans.

After having a bite to eat, Grandma Coco, Karina, and I were on the road by 2:30. We were thankful that we had beaten the evening traffic. Just a few minutes after getting onto the main road, we rounded a corner and hit a huge pothole! After being towed, getting new tires, and filing a complaint at the police department about the pothole, we finally got back on the road and made it home by 9:00 p.m., all for a five-minute CT scan.

In November 2008, Karina stopped crawling and started walking full-time. She also got her first pair of prescription glasses. Her article in the *Ladies' Home Journal* was published in the December issue. It was so much fun to read her story in a real publication. I bought several copies and gave them to Karina's grandparents, her great-grandparents, and some of Karina's doctors.

When the nurse at the ophthalmologist's office first put Karina's glasses on her, she gave us a huge smile, as if things looked amazing to her. Karina did well keeping her glasses on when we were sitting next to her, but if she was alone, and they started to slide down her nose, she would pull them off as quick as a wink. She would also attempt to crumple them in her fist. It was a constant battle to keep her little wire rimmed glasses in decent shape.

One of my favorite memories from December 2008 was looking at the Christmas lights. We would drive around town and enjoy the Christmas decorations. Karina would say, "ooohhh Itty, itty." She thought the lights were pretty. It was so much fun to experience the newness of Christmas decorations with her.

Excerpt from CarePages

January 16, 2009

Karina turned eighteen months old this week. Today, she received her first police report. I went out with a friend to enjoy a very rare, quiet brunch. While I was gone, Britta, who was home with all the kids, called to tell me that the police were coming to our house because Karina had dialed 911 and hung up. I left my friend and my hot breakfast, which had just been served, and raced the sheriff to our house.

I got into the driveway before he did, only because he went past the house to turn around. I had everyone leave the living room except for Britta and Karina. When the sheriff came to the door, he explained that someone at our house had called 911, and Britta pointed to Karina. He just laughed and wrote down her name, her date of birth, my name, my date of birth, and our address. Karina is not only the first person of our family to be on WGN News and to have an article in Ladies' Home Journal, but also the first in our family to be written up by the police for calling 911.

Thanks for reading our posts on CarePages. We continue to covet your prayers. We are so thankful that she is doing well.

In Christ,
Christie for Karina and the rest of the Geaschels

31

"MOM, MORE HELP," KARINA SAID, as she put her first three words together. She was asking for help with her supper. She was nineteen months old, and she was able to say about forty words. As her vocabulary was growing daily and she could now put some words together, we decided to quit speech therapy. The therapist had assured us that Karina did not need to reach this milestone until she was two years old. She was a miracle! Some words were hard for those outside of our family to understand, but we could decipher most of what she said.

One day, one of the kids asked if there was anything more for supper, and I said, "No, that's about it." Karina chimed in, "About it!" The whole family laughed, as this young child who could not communicate for such a long time was copying mom. She repeated it about ten times because she enjoyed our reaction so much. Some of the consonants that we still did not hear were *P* and *C*. She also was not very fluent in the *B* sound, as she would often substitute the *D* sound instead.

In February 2008, Karina, Grandma Coco, Britta, Armin, and I went into Chicago for a photo shoot. Karina was going to be highlighted in the Children's Memorial Hospital newsletter the following month.

The last big news for February was that the family finished paying off the hospital debt that we had incurred since Karina's birth. We had eleven different medical bills that were due each month, and we were diligent to pay them off. We also had a lot of help because of the garage sales that we had held and many donations from family members, friends, and our church family. We were very thankful to pay that debt off and start with a clean financial slate.

Excerpt from CarePages

May 7, 2009

We're still here. Wow, I guess it's been awhile. My life is busy with a newborn (Clara Sylvia Geaschel joined us on March 22, 2009), a toddler, two preschoolers, five homeschooled kids, and a house on the market with showings popping up here and there.

Karina continues to grow and learn. She now weighs twenty-four pounds and still loves to eat. She says new words daily. She can name everyone in the family. She calls Armin "Marnin." Britta is "Bee-ta." Anna is "Naana" And Bill is "Da-dee." I'm usually "Mom." The others are some sort of variation of their name, including Baby Clara who is, "Daa-dee Lara."

Karina taught herself to spin in circles and walk on her tiptoes. She seems to have a very high pain tolerance, which helps when she is outside a lot and scraping her

little legs. We haven't been to any doctors lately, so there
are no updates in that area.

Thank you for continuing to think of us and pray for us.
Karina continues to amaze us.

In Christ,
Christie for the Geaschels Eleven

In June, we met with the plastics' doctor. He thought that Karina looked great. He said that we did not need to come back for another year. Nothing currently needed to be done.

After Karina's appointment, we met my cousin and her daughter at the Lincoln Park Zoo. Karina was at a fun age to take to the zoo. Everything was new and exciting because she had never seen any of it before. For a while, her big sister Britta took her around, showed her everything, and told her what things were called. I loved bringing the entire family into Chicago and making a day trip out of it. It seemed much more worthwhile to do because of the driving and the traffic that we went through.

While we were there at the zoo, we got an unexpected call, telling us that Bill's job was going to end very soon. One of his coworkers called to tell him that someone outside of their shop (one of their vendors) had called and told him that the shop would be closing in the next couple of weeks. It was such a shock, and we wondered what the next chapter in our lives would be. We knew that God was with us, that He went before us, and that He would be there to help us.

32

"DO YOU KNOW WHERE KARINA is," I asked my three oldest girls as they went out to play. They all stopped and looked at me in a funny way. Right near my head, I heard a little voice say, "Here." They started laughing. I had been standing there, clearing and washing the table, while holding Karina, without even realizing it. Over the years, it had been a common occurrence for me to hold someone while I was working and not realize that they were in my arms, but it usually was not someone old enough to answer. I joined them in their laughter and told them that they could go outside and play.

Karina said, "Doing," for, "What are you doing?" She said, "Mine," for anything that belonged to her or if she wondered if it was hers. Karina was also trying out her singing voice. Even though we usually could not understand the words in her songs, her pitch was fairly good. She was known for singing throughout the grocery store, at the top of her lungs, and not caring who was watching or listening to her.

Excerpt from CarePages

August 17, 2009

Last week we moved to the farmhouse. We are still trying to sell the other house, but we figured it would be easier to keep it clean without nine children living in it (not to mention the parents and the cat).

Karina has adjusted well, as she does with any change that our family goes through. She likes to play outside. She loves to tell the chickens to be quiet when the rooster crows. Karina can put three to four words together frequently now, and she still talks constantly. She is a little bundle of energy. No wonder she needs two naps when we are home.

We have no other appointments scheduled at this time. We watch, wait, and thank God that she is doing well.

Thank you all for your prayers, encouragement, thoughts, support, and love over the past two years. We appreciate all of you, and thank God for His goodness to Karina and our family.

In Christ,
Christie for the Geaschels

33

"WE TRUST THAT YOU AND Bill will bring her back if you feel she has any issues with the tumor," the oncology specialists told us. We could not believe what we heard! I thought that they normally kept seeing patients for yearly visits, but they were dismissing Karina because they trusted us with her care.

Karina was not as pleased with the appointment as we were. She did not like any part of the checkup. One would have thought that she was having blood taken, when in all reality, they were only weighing and measuring her. Karina was probably the crabbiest that she had been at any of our appointments. We were not sure if it was because she was not as used to going to appointments anymore or if she was having memories of previous visits.

During this last appointment, we also visited the NICU, but we were only able to see one of the nurses who had taken care of Karina. On our way out of the hospital, we saw one of the nurses who had been at Karina's delivery. Over the previous two years, we had seen this nurse periodically. She would always approach us to find out how Karina was doing. I never recognized her, but she always remembered us and especially Karina.

Excerpt from CarePages

February 4, 2010

It's time for an update. Hello, everyone. We have officially sold our house (closed on it last week), and we are enjoying full-time farm life. We have two German shepherd puppies and chickens. Goats will possibly join us in the spring. Bill is still unemployed, but he is finding odd jobs to keep him busy.

Karina continues to be a bundle of joy. She sings the "Alphabet Song" at the top of her lungs and tries to join in with other songs. She also likes "Old MacDonald Had a Farm." Many Christmas songs are also still in her head. She will sit and look at any book and say, "Look, Jane. See Spot" because she hears Elaina and Greta learning to read their Dick and Jane books.

Karina moved out of her crib and joined six of her sisters in the big-girl room. She recently decided that she should walk up and down the stairs like the rest of the family, instead of sliding down on her bottom.

A few days ago, one of the dogs bumped her in the nose, and it started bleeding like a faucet. I had flashbacks to the days in oncology when her tumor bled uncontrollably. At first, I wondered if the dog bumped the area where the tumor was, but it appears that it was her nose and cheek. It eventually stopped bleeding like those things always do, but we were concerned for a time.

Thanks for taking the time to check up on us.

In Christ,
Christie for Karina and the rest of the Geaschels

CHAPTER

34

"KIDS, KIDS, I WENT POTTY!" Karina yelled each time she used the potty chair. Everyone would then cheer for her and become ecstatic. There were some other new things. Karina loved to bring in the freshly laid eggs and hold the baby chicks. She also liked the job of taking our table scraps to the chickens. She would stand on a stool in the yard as the chickens gathered all around her scrambling for scraps that she was throwing to them.

In April 2010, I was confident that her tumor was completely gone. I could not feel it at all, and her cheek looked much smaller. Karina still loved to sing and talk. She would often make us laugh by saying cute little things.

By the end of May, Karina was mostly potty-trained. She had learned to count to fifteen, and she knew many of her animals when looking at picture books.

Life was busy. We were homeschooling. The children were taking care of all the animals, and we had a large house to keep clean. Bill gradually started his own home-maintenance business, as people kept asking him to do construction jobs. He would usually take one or two of the children with him, depending on the job. Armin would go when it was heavier construction work. Britta would sometimes go with Bill and help people organize or clean things. Sometimes Anna would go and help him paint. It was great for their one-on-one daddy time.

One of the benefits was having him home more hours of the day, even though it was tough financially. We enjoyed being able to eat breakfast as a family and the flexibility of Bill's schedule, which allowed him to join us in activities that he would not have been able to do in the past. At that time, middle-of-the-week trips to zoos, forest preserves, and apple orchards were things that we could all take part in, but before that time, they had been very rare.

Excerpt from CarePages

July 12, 2010

Karina is three years old. Wow! She's three years old. I really can't believe it. Our little miracle baby is three years old.

We never in our wildest dreams thought that she would do this well when we first saw her ultrasounds and talked with her doctors. Some of her specialists didn't think that it was worth their while to give her a helmet for her head's shape because she had so many other problems, consenting only for my sake, not for hers. One of the oncologists told us that one of her chemo drugs would cause learning problems. Her physical therapist in the NICU couldn't get Karina to hold her head straight or look midline. They also didn't think that she would be able to eat while she still had her trach. On and on it goes.

Today at three years old, she talks in complete sentences and paragraphs, runs, jumps, climbs, and turns somersaults. She became potty-trained easier than any of her older siblings and at a younger age than most of them. She sings countless songs. I don't think I need to say more.

Thank you for praying for us and sticking with us for the past three years. We know that the Lord has helped her do all that she can do. We praise Him for her progress, her little life, and all that she has taught us over the past three years.

Because of Christ's love,
Christie for Karina Faith and the Geaschel Family

35

"SHE DOESN'T REALLY HAVE FAVORITES. She loves everything!" I wrote on CarePages, December 5, 2010.

Karina was continuing to grow and learn. She liked to do school with the other kids and felt left out when she couldn't. As a three-and-a-half-year-old, she loved to sing, color, do puzzles, count, draw, and play with her siblings.

By her fourth birthday, we were just starting to go to medical appointments again. Karina's siblings had seen her trying to make the left side of her face smile while standing in front of the mirror.

Around the time that she turned four, we were also referred to a cranial-facial abnormalities clinic in Rockford. Our orthodontist was on the panel of specialists, which also included an audiologist, a speech therapist, a psychologist, an oral surgeon, and a plastic surgeon.

Karina was very shy for the doctors, and she did not want to talk for anyone, including the speech therapist. As we made our rounds to each specialist, he or she asked Karina so many questions and tried so many ways to get her to talk and she would have no part of it. After trying for about 15 minutes, the speech therapists finally did get a small sample of her speech… as we were leaving the room, she started talking freely to me in complete sentences. If it hadn't been so embarrassing, it would have been quite comical.

The audiologist's test was once again inconclusive. Most of the specialists on the panel had no recommendations at that time, except to see her again in a year.

The plastics' surgeon was the only one with a recommendation. He wanted to meet with us again to start thinking about future possibilities for her. We told him that our main goal was to help her smile. We knew that other issues should be covered first, but we wanted him to keep our goal in mind. He was going to start contacting hospitals and doctors to see if he could find someone who would do a nerve transfer for her. He had not done that kind of surgery in years. He only knew of someone in Canada and possibly another specialist in Texas.

There were some other updates. She was really becoming a fish in the water. She loved to swim, and if she had been able to close her left eye better, I would have let her swim without a life jacket on. As it was, the life jacket held her head above the water while still allowing her to swim.

At the age of four, Karina was a very thankful little girl. When we would leave a place, she would say, "Thank you, Mom and Dad, for letting us go." Karina was also very witty for her age. She always had something to say. She still loved to sing and enjoyed helping with food preparation. Karina thrived on farm life and liked to help the older kids with the chickens, geese, and ducks.

Excerpt from CarePages

November 7, 2011

Finally, she had a conclusive hearing test. Today we received the results that we have been trying to get for over four years.

In the NICU, we were told that they couldn't get good readings on Karina's left ear and that we needed to have another test in a future visit to the hospital. We tried many times. Either no one was available to do the test, or she was too wide-awake or too sleepy to get the test done. They never could get a good reading.

When we started speech therapy, we were told to get her hearing checked. I believe that she was between fifteen and eighteen months old when we took her in, and all they could do at that age was test her overall hearing. At that point, they said her hearing was in a normal range.

This summer when we had her at the cranial-facial abnormalities clinic, the audiologist helped her too much, so we didn't really know what Karina could hear and what she couldn't. She also had some inflammation left over in her right ear, which made it hard to test that ear.

Today, we took her to an audiologist through the Rockford Public Schools. The specialist was very thorough, and he did many tests. The right ear tested in the normal range for everything. The left ear was normal for the eardrum function. Everything else shows that there are clearly nerve issues on the left side.

For those who understand pitch and decibels of loudness, she has a mild hearing loss in the five hundred to one thousand frequency range. She can hear thirty decibels or higher. For the two thousand to four thousand frequency range, she can't hear anything until it gets to eighty-five to one hundred decibels or higher. This puts her left ear in the severe-to-profound hearing loss category for higher frequencies.

The audiologist told us that if Karina was attending public school, she would probably need a hearing aid, but because she was homeschooled, she should do OK. We are going to pay closer attention to when she can hear us and when she can't so that we can determine if we need to get her a hearing aid.

I am so thankful to finally get some results and to know that there is an issue so that we can help her better. We are thankful that her right ear is perfectly fine, which has helped her tremendously in learning to communicate with all of us.

Here is a little update on the rest of the family: I have been on bed rest since August 4. My C-section is scheduled for September 23. I don't have much longer to wait to see if Karina will have another sister or a brother.

Karina's next appointment is in October. She will be seeing the plastic surgeon to determine if he can transfer some of the nerves on the right side of her face to the left side.

Love,
Christie

CHAPTER

36

"FOR NOW, WE WILL ENJOY the year of her being four, and we will not have to make big decisions for her future," I reported to CarePages, December 27, 2011.

Karina had recently been back to the plastic surgeon. We had learned about the different options that we had to choose from. We also were in the deciding phases of whether we should get a hearing aid. She needed the music in the van to be very loud, and still she could not hear or understand most of the words to the songs. She sang along, but her words didn't usually make sense. She also did not always hear us if she was outside and we were calling her to come inside the house.

On another note, the ophthalmologist was pleasantly surprised with her eyes looking so well. He wanted her to continue to wear her glasses, but Karina could not decide if they helped her, so it was always a struggle to keep them on her.

Karina had become a big sister once again. Baby Tia Jubilee had been born in September, and at three months old, she was still quite the novelty of the house. All the children loved her, doted on her, and totally enjoyed having another baby around. At four and a half years old, Karina still loved to color, sing, look at books, and play house with Little People and Playmobil.

Birthday Excerpt from CarePages

July 13, 2012

She's five years old! I can't believe it's been five years since Karina's birth. She is such a miracle. The past six months have been ones of change.

Karina got her hearing aid this spring, and it is a great help. Even the day she got it, she noticed right away that she could hear her voice in both ears instead of just in her right ear. She does well with it, and she enjoys decorating it with stickers.

We also had another meeting with the cranial-facial abnormalities group in Rockford. There are some interesting decisions that we will be making in the future. We, as her parents, are most interested in trying to fix the nerves in the left side of her face so that she can use the muscles on both sides.

The plastic surgeon in Rockford recommended doing all structural or skin surgeries first (so as not to mess up the nerves after transferring them). The orthodontist and oral surgeons said that the jawbone could not be worked on until she is done growing (about sixteen years old). If we can't do anything to the jaw until she is done growing, and can't do anything to the nerves until the jaw heals, we ultimately can't do anything for years.

I am of the understanding that the nerves will have a better chance of working if we do something sooner rather than later. We will make a fall appointment for a CT scan in Chicago. Then we can meet again with her original plastic surgeon in Chicago and see what his thoughts are. There are still lots of questions.

Karina loves to sing, especially with her siblings. She still likes to color and do puzzles. She has not yet caught on to reading, but she loves to be read to.

She never asks about her face. I do not know if I should bring it up with her or wait for her to ask. She knows that she had a tumor at birth, that she was in the hospital for a long time, and that a lot of people were and still are praying for her. She loves to look at pictures of when she was a baby.

On the home front, things were not crazy enough for us, so we bought a gutted house and two acres of land. We are working on rebuilding it and hoping to move in before winter. (That is a story for another book).

Britta, Karina's oldest sister, has her driver's license now. Her baby sister, Tia, is crawling and pulling herself up by holding onto the furniture. Everyone else falls somewhere in the middle.

Thank you for still checking up on us and for your prayers.

In Christ,
The Geaschel Dozen

In October 2012, Karina had another CT scan. This was her first scan since she was eighteen months old. The appointment was at the brand-new Lurie Children's Hospital. It had recently been finished, and all the patients and doctors had moved to the new building. The new facility was directly across the street from the Prentice Women's Hospital, where I had delivered Karina. The two hospitals were also connected by a skywalk. Now when a baby is transferred to Children's Hospital, the moms from Prentice can more easily go and visit. I know that when I was a patient at Prentice, I would have loved the opportunity to be closer to Karina, when she was at Children's Hospital.

The new building is beautiful and child friendly. Karina did great at her scan. For quite some time, we had been practicing lying very still in different positions. She was now old enough to be scanned without sedation.

The hardest part of the trip was that they did not warn us that some of her scans needed to be taken with contrast. That meant that they needed to insert an IV to get the dyes into her veins. She did great, but it took quite a while to find a good vein. After the first prolonged attempt, they had to re-prep and try again. Bill was the one who really struggled with the needles, and almost became a patient himself.

After we were finally done, we gathered up all of our other children from the waiting room and headed over to the Lincoln Park Zoo. After our full day, we went home to await the CT results.

37

"THE TUMOR THAT YOU HAD when you were born ruined the muscles and the nerves in your face, and that is why the left side doesn't work right," I said to Karina. She was five and a half years old when I was finally able to explain that to her.

At the time that I finally talked to her about her facial muscles, we were staying at my parent's house while rebuilding our new house. I had sent Karina to the bathroom to wait for me, so that I could fix her hair. When I came into the bathroom, I found her making faces at herself in the mirror. I asked her what she was doing, and she showed me that she could wink with one eye, while keeping the other one completely still. Of course, she could not do the reverse.

I went on to explain that the reason we had been visiting so many doctors was that we had been trying to find the right ones to help her. We wanted her to be able to wink and smile with both sides of her face.

When I asked her about her thoughts, she said, "I like being able to wink with just one eye." Then she walked over to the sink so that I could fix her hair.

I was so thankful that God had brought about this conversation in a natural way. I was glad that I had not pushed the conversation earlier, when I thought it should happen, but I had waited until she initiated it. After that, she continued to show people how she could wink with one eye, without the other eye moving at all. She seemed to be proud of her newfound skill.

Excerpt from CarePages

January 16, 2013

The doctors want to move forward. I think that this is the first time in five years that we are moving toward surgery for Karina. We have been in a wait-and-see stage for so long that I'm not sure how to feel right now. Should I feel excited or scared for her? Do I just want to keep things the way that they are? We saw the orthodontist last week to get his opinion about her jaw and teeth before our appointment this week with the plastics' surgeon at Lurie Children's Hospital. The orthodontist, Bill, and I agreed that according to the CT scan and the panoramic x-ray that the orthodontist had just taken, it wouldn't harm her to reconstruct the malformed left jawbone. The only tooth that showed up in the back of her mouth, on the lower left side, was a twelve-year molar. It was coming in sideways and was not near her other teeth. Furthermore, it was also not interfering with the part of the jaw that needed reconstruction.

Yesterday, we took the family into Chicago for Karina's appointment with the plastic surgeon. He stated that he would like to see something done sooner rather than later. He knows that we are most interested in a nerve transplant to help the left side work as it should. We also agree that before that can be done, there has to be some reconstruction to make a firm foundation for the nerves. After performing the nerve transfer, it might take up to two years before we know if it has worked. It is a very complex surgery, and it takes a long time for the nerves to regenerate.

We now have a referral to see an oral surgeon, who will then be in touch with the plastic surgeon. Together, they will make a plan of action, which Bill and I will look over to decide if it is a path that we want to use for her.

Please pray for wisdom for the doctors, Bill, and me so that we will make the right decisions for Karina. As Christians, it's hard to find the balance between helping our daughter accepting that this is how she has been created, and knowing what steps to take to intervene during the whole process.

When Karina had had the CT scan last fall, we had not prepared her ahead of time for the IVs. Then when we went to the orthodontist and she had the panoramic x-ray done, we also had not prepared her ahead of time. So she was a little uncertain of this doctor's appointment. She did fine when they weighed and measured her, but she started to cry when they wanted to take her blood pressure. She wondered what it all meant and what else they were going to do to her. She was relieved when they said that they only wanted to talk to her, touch her face, and have her make faces at them.

Her plastic surgeon sees hundreds of kids each year. When we first came into his office, he looked at her for a minute and then said, "Oh, I remember you." I reminded him of the helmet that she had worn when she had been a baby. He told the assistant that no one else thought he should use the helmet because of the severity of her issues, but he had wanted to do it anyway. As I remember the story, he used the helmet for my sake because he knew that it was a way to allow me to feel like I was helping her.

Again as always, thank you for your prayers during the past five-plus years and for keeping up with CarePages. Most of our followers thought that when we went home from the hospital, our CarePages would stop, but it was just the beginning for her.

Love,
Christie for the Geaschel Dozen

Over the next months, we finally met with the oral surgeon who had been recommended by the plastic surgeon at Lurie Children's in Chicago. He told us that he thought the surgery should not happen soon. This was so disappointing for us, and we did not know what to do at that point. I tried to contact Karina's plastic surgeon to see what he thought should be done. When I reached his office, they told me that he no longer worked at Lurie Children's Hospital.

I thought, *What? How could he leave when he was finally going to do something?* It was so hard to even begin to explain what I was feeling at that point. They told me the name of the hospital where he now worked, but I decided that I didn't want to follow him to a new hospital. Since the oral surgeon that he had worked with was not interested in helping Karina anytime soon, we didn't see a reason to go to his new hospital. We were at a loss as to what to do. I talked to family and friends, and told them of our dilemma, asking them for their advice and prayers. A good friend of mine mentioned that we should see if Shriners Hospital could help us. I was not really sure how to get into a hospital like that, but I decided to try and see what would happen. The answer was already a "no" unless I would ask, right?

I found Shriners Hospital online and read that among other issues, they specialized in helping cleft-palate patients. Thinking that some of Karina's issues were similar, I decided to contact them and see what would happen. I looked around on their website, found an email address, and typed out a brief but thorough summary of Karina's life. I sent it and then waited. After a day or two, they responded and gave us an appointment at their Chicago office. I couldn't believe how easy it was! I didn't need a physician's referral or past records. I only needed to email them and show up with Karina for an appointment.

During the summer of 2013, we met with the craniofacial surgeon at Shriners. A lot of his time was spent listening to Karina's story, and he asked many questions. He did a very thorough exam and introduced the other people on the team: a photographer (who did a complete photo shoot), a nurse (who asked almost as many questions as the surgeon), and a therapist (who talked to us and to Karina, as she tried to find if there were any underlying needs that hadn't yet been expressed).

After the exam, he told us that he really wanted to help Karina, and help her soon, but that he couldn't help her with the resources that he had at Shriners. He also worked at the University of Illinois at Chicago (UIC) hospital, which was located in the downtown medical district in Chicago. He wanted us to visit his other team of specialists there.

When we got home, I called UIC and made a new appointment, and after a couple of months, we visited him there. He took more pictures of her and sent her across the street to get a CT scan. We were so surprised that we could get her in for a scan right then and there. After the scan, we went back to his office, and he went over everything with us.

The surgeon needed a few weeks to figure out the way that he would proceed with the surgery and bone reconstruction, which we had scheduled for the following November. We told Karina about the surgeon's plans, and she seemed to understand the minimal details that we gave her. It was exciting and a bit scary to think that her surgery was finally scheduled. We had always known and planned for a future surgery, ever since we discovered that she had a tumor, even before her birth.

Excerpt from CarePages

November 9, 2013

Surgery number one is complete. Karina had her first bone reconstruction done today (Friday) at the UIC. She did wonderfully! The surgery was supposed to last three to four hours. After two hours, the doctor called and asked to see us.

Bill and I talked on the way up to the OR. We wondered the reason why the surgeon could possibly want to talk to us in the middle of the surgery. Was she OK? Was she bleeding too much? Was he unable to do the surgery? We prayed, talked, and then waited for him. We did not know what he wanted.

After waiting an agonizing fifteen minutes for the surgeon to join us, he arrived with a smile and told us that surgery was over, that there was no incision on the outside of the face, and that she could possibly go home the next day.

She had had pain on and off, but she was doing well.

Even with all the swelling that was caused by her surgery, it is amazing to see her mouth midline instead of shifted to the right.

Thank you for your continued prayers.

Love,
Christie for Karina Faith

That fifteen-minute wait for the surgeon had been awful. We never expected the surgery to be over in half the amount of time that had been suggested. Our oldest daughter, Britta, and my cousin were with us in the waiting room when we got the message to meet with the surgeon, so they knew that they needed to pray for the meeting. The walk to the elevator, the ride up, and the wait in the meeting room seemed to take forever. Bill and I went over every possible scenario that we could, wondering why he was meeting with us.

When the surgeon came quickly into the room and delivered his ten-second speech, we were in shock. We couldn't believe that it was really over, that there were no incisions on the outside, and that we'd be going home the next day. Karina and I had a few changes of clothes with us because I thought that we would possibly be there for three to four days.

After this first surgery, Karina was an interesting patient while in the hospital. She tried talking to me as soon as she was awake. We could not understand what she was saying, because her whole head was wrapped in gauze. She kept trying to tell me, "You forgot. You forgot." I finally figured out that she was saying that the shirt that I told her she could wear in the hospital was not on her yet. It was a pretty, pink, crew neck shirt that had the words, "Treat me like a princess," on it. We thought it would be a good hospital shirt, but I never thought that she would expect to put it on right after surgery, especially since her head was wrapped up with gauze and the IVs were still in her hands.

Karina also wanted to be very independent in the hospital, so the nurses decided to give her a rubber syringe to feed herself various liquids, as it was too hard for her to drink from a spoon or a cup. She became attached to some beautiful flowers that my cousin had brought for her. Karina wanted to sleep with the flowers, even though she knew it meant that they would not last very long. She and her roses were inseparable.

We went home from the hospital after only twenty-four hours. She was glad to be home, but she went through a time of depression. I was not sure if it was the surgery's drugs leaving her system or something else. We were glad when we saw that our little girl was back to herself after a few days.

Karina had to keep the gauze wrap on for just a couple of days. Then she used a bib for a few days to catch the drainage that came from her mouth. Later that week, it was hard to keep her in bed because she was feeling so much better. Karina had almost no pain, and she did not want to sit any longer. Two days after being home, she surprised us by going upstairs by herself to play with her sisters. She then also joined us at the table for breakfast and lunch.

For a few days, she was on a liquid/mush diet, but she increased her intake daily, even though the surgeon had taken out the parts of her jawbone that had been deformed. Although Karina had quite a few stitches in her mouth, she was back to eating raw carrots within a couple of weeks. The main goal of that first reconstruction was to make the left side of her face look structurally more like the right side. I was in awe of the fact that they could remove some of her jawbone from the inside of the mouth with only a minor incision.

During that year, she was able to swim and read better, and she learned to ride her bike. She still loved to sing. Our family started to share our musical talents at various places around town. Sometimes Karina would sing a short solo if she knew the words well. We would go to a rescue mission in our town for homeless men and women and share the devotional during the evening meal. We also visited nursing homes and sang for a couple of evening services at my parents' church. Most of the time that we rode in the van, the girls would burst into song.

The summer that Karina turned seven years old, 2014, her oldest sister, Britta, was married. It was a busy spring and summer as our family frequently got together with the family of the soon-to-be groom. Their courtship quickly turned into an engagement.

During the summer, our family also went on a fifteen-day trip, partly to learn about the history of our country and partly as a missions' trip. We first visited the Creation Museum in Kentucky and then drove to South Carolina. For the mission trip part of our time away, we went to Hilton Head Island, SC and helped with a vacation Bible school at a local church, joined a beach ministry, visited a nursing home where we sang and painted with the Alzheimer's patients, as well as helping with various other tasks that we were asked to do.

One of our favorite things was filling backpacks with Bibles, nonperishable food, and bottles of water. Then we walked around a neighborhood where the people seemed to be in need, and handed out the backpacks. Bill walked up to each house, talked to the adults, and explained that we had come from Illinois to pray with and for the people in their neighborhood. People let him pray for them, and they were glad to receive the backpacks from us.

After the missions trip, we visited Jamestown, Virginia, and Yorktown. Then we drove to Chincoteague Island in Virginia to celebrate Greta's tenth birthday and see the wild ponies. From there, we drove to Gettysburg, Pennsylvania, and then headed west and north.

The last part of the trip was spent on Mackinac Island, Michigan, where Bill and I had gone for our honeymoon. We were celebrating our twentieth anniversary, so we wanted the kids to see the wonderful place where we had gone after our wedding. We had a great time as a family. We were so thankful that all twelve of us had the opportunity to go before Britta had her big day and moved with her husband one and a half hours away.

Britta's wedding day was perfect. The weather was warm but not hot. It was cloudy but not raining. The theme was country western: cowboy boots, cowgirl hats, and fiddle music for the processional and recessional. Karina was one of the junior bridesmaids, and all the other siblings were in the wedding party, too. The kids recited 1 Corinthians 13 and then sang. It was a fun day and a wonderful celebration of the joining of a new family.

It was also a very sad day for Karina. Her big sister was getting married. Britta had been Karina's "big buddy" since her birth, and it was a hard adjustment for a few months. As time went by, Karina became used to Britta being gone, but she really looked forward to visiting her sister and her new brother at their home. Once in a while, Britta let her siblings spend the night. That was a favorite activity of Karina's.

During the summer that Karina turned 7, the orthodontist decided that it was time to make a retainer for Karina. He told us that because no teeth had come in on the bottom left side, there was nothing to keep the top teeth from growing down too far. The retainer that he made had extra plastic on it and acted like the bottom left molars. She took care of it fairly well, but it was not long before we had to order a new one. She had been outside with her sisters, and they and some friends were eating beans out of the garden. Of course, Karina took out the retainer, and then it was gone. We looked all over and even used a borrowed metal detector, but the retainer was nowhere to be found.

Karina adjusted well the months after the first surgery, and it was not long before we visited her surgeon so that we could figure out the next step in her care. After visiting him in the early fall, he made a surgery appointment for November. This time, the focus was on getting everything midline. Now that the bone was out of the way and her jaw was more symmetrical, he felt that doing a major face-lift would move her face midline. Currently, her mouth was on the right side of her face, and we could not even see her middle teeth unless we moved her cheek to look inside her mouth. Karina was not too concerned with the thought of another surgery in the near future.

38

"DO YOU THINK IT WOULD be possible to go home today?" we hesitantly asked the surgeon when we first arrived at the hospital. It was November 3, 2014, and it was the day of surgery number two. Karina had been prepped and we had already spoken with the anesthesiologist and told her of Karina's main concerns, and gotten those things resolved. Then the nurse told us to ask the surgeon if we could go home that same day since Karina's last surgery had gone so well. When we asked the surgeon, he agreed that she would heal much better at home. He would check back with us after the surgery.

Excerpt from CarePages

November 3, 2014

Wow! Surgery started at 1:14 p.m. At 2:50, they were finishing up. Everything had gone well. About 4:20, we were on our way home! She had only lost about two teaspoons of blood.

Thank you for your prayers.

Love,
Christie

The surgery went better than expected. The anesthesiologist had helped to alleviate the issues that Karina had had from the previous surgery. When Karina thought about that first experience, the only thing she complained about was the stickers that had been used to keep the probes on. Because Karina had been a bit uncomfortable right after surgery, the nurse had not taken them off before we had been discharged. We had tried on and off for about a week to get them removed. We finally put olive oil on them and had her soak in the tub. In Karina's memory, those stickers caused more pain than the bone surgery had caused. It was the thing that she most dreaded when facing another procedure.

This time, the anesthesiologist told us that she would remove the stickers before Karina was awake, and she did. Karina was greatly relieved. I was also able to be right by Karina's side before she was even awake. When I asked the nurse if it would be a few hours before we would be able to go home, she said, "No, you can go home in about an hour." I was shocked because Karina was not even awake yet.

As Karina started to wake up, the nurse gave her some juice, took out her IVs, and had Bill go get her clothes so that we could get her ready to go home. As we were leaving the hospital, Karina was still half-asleep. It was wonderful that she slept the whole way home. It was during a busy traffic time of day, and if she had been awake, it would have been painful for her as we stopped and started so frequently.

Once we were home, she went through another short time of depression but then came out of it and healed quickly. A couple of weeks later, the surgeon, Bill, and I were all a bit discouraged with the results of the surgery. He had gotten everything midline. It had looked great while she had been asleep after the surgery, but because of gravity and no working muscles, when she stood up, the skin and muscles had seemed to move back to where they had been.

A few more weeks went by. As the swelling dissipated, and she had healed considerably more, we could see that there actually was quite a bit of progress in how her facial structure had improved since before the surgery. I could see Karina's middle teeth when she smiled instead of the teeth on the right side of her mouth, and she could now whistle. She'd never been able to make her lips do that. Karina also noticed that she could open her mouth more fully than before surgery.

When we went for one of her post-op checkups, the surgeon mentioned that in the following spring, we could possibly meet with a team of surgeons back at Shriners Hospital, who performed surgeries where they transferred tendons from the arm to the mouth. The tendon would be attached to the nerves from the corner of her mouth to a place near her ear. Eventually, it would help her to smile. It was exciting to think that we might not have to wait until Karina was a teen before seeing her smile.

In the following spring, the plastic surgeon said that he had met a new surgeon who did nerve transfers for patients in the Chicago area. In the fall, we would see him again and find out what was next for our little Karina Faith.

39

"WE TREAT THE PATIENTS HERE like family. If I'm not comfortable enough to do this surgery on my own child, I won't do it on yours," the new surgeon told us. It was October 2015, and we were finally meeting the micro cranial-facial surgeon, who was planning to give Karina a smile.

I had taken Karina and her big sister Greta back to Shriners Hospital so that we could finally meet the surgeon whom the plastics surgeon had told us about the previous spring. The appointment went well, and we were told, "Come back in a few months." That would give Bill and me time to talk about things and the surgeon time to consult with his colleagues in Texas and Canada. Only a handful of microsurgeons worked with plastics, and Karina's new surgeon was on the cutting edge of this new technology (pun intended).

In January 2016, we went back to visit Shriners Hospital. This time

Bill was able to take the day off work. Once again, we brought Greta with us to the appointment. Karina liked to have a sibling with her for hospital day trips. She liked to show her sisters the playroom. When it was warm outside, they spent time on the playground. They also usually went home with some kind of special gift given by the hospital.

The surgeon explained the three different types of nerve-transfer surgeries that were currently being used. We decided on one that had only been around for two years. This surgeon had only been in Chicago for the previous six months, and we were so thankful that God had put him there to help Karina. Sure, we could have gone to Texas or Canada, but having someone placed within an hour or two of home was perfect. We were in awe of the way that God orchestrated everything.

Excerpt from CarePages

January 2016

A year ago, we were told of a surgeon who might be able to help Karina smile. The tendon surgery, which we first had been told about, would have given her a permanent smirk (half-smile). Instead, the micro-cranial facial surgeon, who we recently met, wants to transfer a thin muscle in her leg to her left cheek. The muscle, veins, and nerves would all need to be plugged into working ones, so this is a very delicate and long surgery. Karina would probably be in the hospital for seven to ten days to make sure that everything is working properly.

As I've been considering this surgery, I've spoken to some of her other surgeons and her orthodontist. I want to make sure that they feel it's necessary and not only a cosmetic, frivolous surgery. They all gave reasons why this would be beneficial. The main reason is that her facial muscles have atrophied, and her mouth is getting smaller. Her mouth muscles will continue to atrophy, unless she can start opening it on the left side.

I'd like her to have the surgery while it's still cold out and while the kids aren't outside much because after surgery, Karina will have to be very careful for a while. I don't want to limit her summertime activity.

Please keep us and the surgeon in your prayers. Pray that this surgery would be the right path to take and for wisdom for all who are involved. We have been praying about being able to help her smile since she was four years old.

Thank you and God bless you,

Christie for the rest of the flock of Geaschels

The surgery was to be scheduled within the next couple of months. On our end, Karina had to have a complete physical check up by her pediatrician to clear her for surgery. After that, paperwork would be sent to Shriners so that the date could be scheduled.

Back at home, life went on as normal (whatever that was). Homeschooling, neighborhood craft nights for the girls organized by Anna and Eva, orthodontist appointments, church activities, and various other events kept our family of eleven busy.

40

"I THINK IT WILL BE good to be able to smile." Karina stated when I asked her about the upcoming surgery. Her procedure was scheduled for April 19 at 6:00 a.m. When I asked Karina what she thought about the surgery, she said, "I don't want that red medicine that they give me so I will get sleepy". That is when she told me about the awful tasting medicine that she had been given before her last two surgeries. I told her that there were other ways to get kids sleepy. "The doctors can give you a mask with air blowing through it. I'm sure you'd do good with that. Another option is to use an IV, which you also tolerate well. Some kids don't like masks or IVs, so the doctors had to come up with a medicine for those kids. We will definitely find another way to get you to sleep," I reassured her. That ended our surgery talk, and we went on with other daily activities.

Karina had finally reached an age that our family thought was old enough to care for a pet. She chose a bunny. Caring for her bunny taught her many things: caring for something besides herself (even in the snow or the rain), saving money so that she could buy its food, and learning how to safely hold it so that she and the bunny would not be harmed. She also had to spend time with it so that it would become tame.

41

"COULD WE SPEND THE NIGHT before surgery at your house?" I asked my cousin who lived in downtown Chicago. The weeks progressed, and finally, the day before surgery arrived. We again headed into Chicago and spent the night with my cousin and her family. They only lived about seven miles away from Shriners Hospital. It was a great place to stay, since we had to arrive at the hospital by 6:00 a.m. We enjoyed catching up with each other and eating some late-night snacks, knowing that Karina would not be eating real food for a while and that she would be sleeping the whole next day, during and after surgery. Karina played with my cousin's children while Bill and I talked with the adults.

Karina slept well, and she eagerly got up the morning of surgery. She still showed no signs of apprehension, and she remained at peace while we gathered all of our things and prepared to head to the hospital. Bill and I made sure that we had eaten before Karina got up, so as not to make her want to eat. A couple of times that morning, I told her that she could eat or at least drink something on the following day.

We arrived at the hospital in good time, and we were checked in. The staff members who we met with were very helpful and encouraging, which set a nice tone for that early in the morning.

One of the surgical students came into Karina's pre-op room with a permanent marker and asked Karina to smile. The student was there to trace her natural smile lines on the working right side of the face. She told us that they could not make her smile during surgery, so they had to do it ahead of time. She then drew a matching smile line on the left side of her face so that they would be able to surgically make the same smile lines to match the right side. We told the nurses about Karina's desire not to have the sleepy medicine. They gave Karina her options and said that she would have to decide how she was going to fall asleep. Although she was not crazy about any of the options and it took her awhile to decide, she chose to get the IV while she was awake and get the sleepy medicine through that, before heading into the Operating Room (OR).

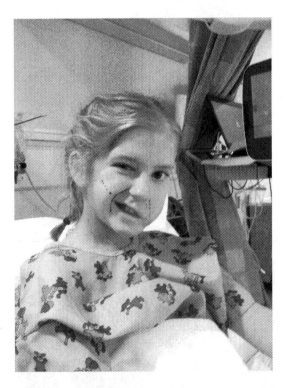

To get the IV into place, the nurse gave Karina an iPad to distract her while they were inserting it. She did so well that she even received two special stuffed animals from the staff. One at a time, the surgical team members made their way into the pre-op room, introduced themselves to us, and went over what was about to take place. Bill asked the surgeon if he could pray with him, and he was assured that it would be very much appreciated. After Bill prayed, the surgeon recited some Bible verses and reassured us that he would treat Karina as if she was his own daughter.

Karina was a bit sad when they started to take her into the OR. She had thought that I would be going with her. We were encouraged by staff members that she would not remember those feelings because she had already received the sleepy medicine. Staff members got our cell-phone numbers and told us that they would call every two hours during the surgery and that we could go make ourselves at home.

Bill and I left to spend some time together, and then Britta joined us for the day. We had our meals together, played some games, had time to sit and talk, and most importantly, spent time in prayer. I also updated CarePages and Facebook pages, texts, and emails as soon we received the frequent phone updates from the OR nurses. We knew that there were so many family members and friends praying for her that we had the freedom to find other things to occupy our minds, to help the day go faster, and to not have to be in worry mode all day. Karina was in God's hands, and we trusted Him with her care.

The surgery started about 8:30 a.m., and we finally received the long-awaited call from the surgeon around 6:00 p.m. He told us that some very difficult procedures had been done on her but that everything had gone smoothly. We would be able to see her soon. Surgery had finished about twelve hours from when we had arrived at the hospital, but she hadn't been in surgery for more than nine and a half hours.

CHAPTER

42

"IS IT TOMORROW?" THESE WERE Karina's first words to us when we met her in the ICU after surgery. I asked her why she was wondering if it was tomorrow, and she sadly said, "I'm so hungry." She remembered that I had told her that she would not be able to eat at all that day, but on the next day (tomorrow), she'd be able to start having something to eat. It was so hard telling her that it was still Tuesday and that she would not be able to have anything for a while. First, her tummy had to wake up, and then she would have to start with ice, juice, and other clear liquids for a while.

She did not have much pain after the surgery-only when the nurses used a Doppler device on her cheek to make sure that they could hear the blood flowing in her new muscle. Her biggest complaint was her empty tummy. Cartoons on the hospital TV helped her pass the hours in the ICU. Bill would go to the cafeteria to get food for him and me so that I was able to stay right with her the entire time, usually holding her hand. Bill and I took turns sitting by her, and we all enjoyed a visit by the hospital's therapy dog.

She looked different right away, even though the nerve and muscle would not work for quite a while. The blue lines that they had drawn on her face before her surgery were still there, and they made her new smile creases so visible. Also, since the swelling had not started yet, we could anticipate how things were going to look in the near future.

Excerpt from CarePages

Wednesday Morning, April 20, 2016

During the night, Karina and I slept well, in between hourly, automatic blood-pressure cuff noises and the nurses also coming in hourly to check Karina's vitals and to listen to her new cheek muscle with a Doppler device.

Karina's biggest complaint has been her hunger. She only got ice chips throughout the night. Finally this morning, she got some apple juice. Her late-night snack on Monday was a long time ago. Progress is good. TVs on the wall are good too. Today we hope that her catheter will be removed and that she will get out of the PICU.

Thanks for your prayers, texts, and phone calls.

Love,
Christie

About twenty hours after getting out of surgery, Karina was moved out of the ICU and into her own room. It was the same room that Britta, Bill, and I had used the day before, and Bill had slept in it the night that Karina was in the ICU. The room was large. It had a bed for her and one for me. There were also five chairs in the room and a couple of tables. We had our own bathroom with a toilet, sink, and shower. It was spacious and quiet, and it had a beautiful view of a secluded park-like setting.

Karina was encouraged to start using her leg and walking to the bathroom right away, but at that point, she was content to be lifted in and out of her wheelchair and bed. Regarding her meals, she wanted to do everything on her own. I just grabbed a large towel and laid it on her, from her chin down to her lap, and let her eat. She would have the IVs attached to her arms for a while, which made eating very tricky. Also, her mouth was not in the exact position as it had been, and it was not moving exactly like it had done before surgery. But all in all, most of the food made it to her mouth.

Excerpt from CarePages

Evening, April 20, 2016

OK, so only twenty-five hours after her surgery, she is in her own room and off all monitors and IVs. She went to the cafeteria with us to eat supper and fed herself (mashed potatoes, collard greens, cottage cheese, and bananas in pudding). Now she is sitting in bed, sipping on her Sprite. Praise God, she is doing great! Thanks for your prayers.

Love,
Christie

43

"YOU CAN'T GET THE DRAIN taken out of your leg until you walk, and you can't go home until you get the drain out of your leg. Let me put it to you plainly. You have to walk in order to go home," the surgeon's intern (Fellow) told Karina. There, he said it. The Fellow who had been at the surgery was doing his rounds when he came in and told Karina the important key of getting out of the hospital.

His little motivational speech made a big difference. She decided to walk to the bathroom. About eight more times that day, she walked. The first time she was a bit apprehensive, and she wanted to walk on her tiptoes, because using her left leg was painful; after I encouraged her to walk normally, she was fine. It was tricky to carry the drain bag with us each time we went to the bathroom, but after we found that the bag fit neatly into her robe's pocket, it became much easier.

Karina and I enjoyed sitting together and talking. Much of the time,

I let her watch cartoons while I did sudoku puzzles. She had been given crafts to do while at the hospital, but with IVs in both of her hands, it restricted her enough that she didn't really want to do much of anything.

She was given her breakfast and lunch in her room, but at supper, the patients went through the cafeteria line and could choose their own food. It was fun to go through the line together, choosing what we wanted for supper. I pushed her in the wheelchair, and she carefully held the tray on her lap.

We brought our supper back to the room. Then as we were about to start eating, we heard over the hospital's loudspeaker that there were some juggling acrobats in the main mall area, so we quickly grabbed our food and headed down to see them. Many other patients were also watching the acrobats with their parents. It was a lot of fun and a great way to enjoy our supper. The husband-and-wife team was amazing, as they balanced each other, juggled, and did all sorts of complicated acts.

The next morning (Friday), three days after her surgery, the surgeon removed the leg drain and gave us the go-ahead to go home. We were excited to be able to take Karina home to finish healing with our family instead of in the hospital, where she would have still been awakened every few hours to be checked on.

Bill left work and came to the hospital right away. He arrived by 10:00 a.m. By the time we were discharged, it was about 11:30. We were home by 1:00 p.m. As we pulled into the driveway, Karina said, "I guess I can't ride my bike yet, right?" After laughing, I agreed with her.

It had been only three days since her surgery. She had just had a muscle removed from her leg and implanted in her face. She had had no pain meds since the previous night. Now she was asking us if she could ride her bike. *Really?* I wondered. I realized, then and there, that it was going to be difficult to keep her down and resting. I secretly wondered why I had been so eager to get her home.

I got Karina settled before I called her sisters at the neighbors' house and told them to come home. Karina was feeling much better, and she was ready to start on all her fun crafts. She seemed to enjoy her time alone with her new things before having to share them with her sisters. Once the other girls arrived home, she was very happy to see them, to tell them all about her hospital stay, and to share her new crafts, toys, and stuffed animals.

It was great to be home. Her sisters had made the sunroom nice and cozy for her. They made the futon into a bed, and it looked comfortable. It had her favorite blankets and pillows all laid out nicely. Karina and I slept there on her first night home so that I could help her get to the bathroom when necessary. I planned to have her sisters take turns sleeping with her, but I thought that I should be with her the first night to make sure she was OK.

Over the next few days, she continued to get stronger, but her face continued to swell more and more. The weather was beautiful, so she was able to sit outside with the cats. Sometimes her sisters would bring her bunny, Sugar Maple, to hold. I did my best to keep her quiet and not too active, but Mom can only do so much. As she felt better, she wanted to rest less and less. As her face continued to swell more, she wanted to see people less and less. She became embarrassed by the way that she looked. She especially did not want people her age to come visit her.

Excerpt from CarePages

April 27, 2016

She got her stitches out today. It went better than I had anticipated. When we arrived at the front desk, the receptionist handed Karina two pieces of mail that had arrived after she was discharged. That was fun for her.

The doctor who removed the stitches did a wonderful job of talking Karina through it. Even though it was painful, she sat still the entire time. We will go back again next week to see the surgeon.

Our biggest prayer request at this point is that Karina would feel better about seeing people. She is embarrassed because of the swelling in her face, and she doesn't want to see anyone.

Love, Christie for Karina

44

"I SAW THE STAPLE IN your photos, and I should have warned you it was in there," the surgeon explained to us. We were in the clinic for Karina's two-week post-op checkup, and I was really feeling scared.

For the past two weeks as Karina's face had continued to swell, the incision area had been opening up. First, the drain hole started stretching. Next, two new little holes near the drain hole opened. Lastly, after about a week, the three holes stretched open to make one big hole. I took pictures daily to document. I kept wondering what I was doing wrong and wondering when we would be taking Karina back in for surgery to fix the new opening in her face.

Even before we left home for her two week post-op appointment, I had packed some extra clothes for both of us. I also had not given Karina much food for breakfast, in case they wanted to take her right in for surgery to fix the huge opening.

I had sent pictures to the resident doctor a few times a day so that they could keep up with what was happening to her. They were not as disturbed as I was. They said that it looked OK and that it had no signs of infection.

By the time we got to the appointment, a shiny staple could be seen inside the opening in Karina's face. I thought it was probably supposed to be there, but my fear was that something else had gotten in there and that I should have tried to get it out of the incision area. At the appointment, the surgeon reassured us that it was supposed to be there and that it was holding a vein in place. He had seen it days earlier in the photos that I had sent, but he had not explained to us that we might be seeing it soon.

Excerpt from CarePages

May 3, 2016

At the two-week post-op appointment, the surgeon assured us that everything was going to be OK. Because of the fact that she had stitches in the same area as she had for her last surgery, the skin there was very thin. When her cheek swelled up, that was the area of least resistance. Everything's healing from the inside, and as long as we can keep it clean and moist, it will do well. He said that we should keep watching for infection and that she should still be very careful not to be injured in that area but that she doesn't have to be on bed rest. After her appointment, we had a good lunch there at the hospital and then headed home with a happy eight-year-old and a much-relieved mommy.

Thank you so much for your prayers.
Christie

That two-week appointment was the climax of the problems. After that, the hole started to heal. As I changed the dressing daily and cleaned and added moisture, it was a relief to see the wound healing. It was another two weeks before the hole was healed enough so that Karina could start to wear her glasses again. It was hard for her to get used to them again, as she hadn't worn them since the day of her surgery. She also was not able to wear her hearing aid during her healing time, as the incision and then the post-surgery opening were both right at the front and top of her ear.

Some family and friends sent Karina wonderful notes and cards, encouraging her in everything that she went through. One friend in particular had explained about some struggles that she had had as a child, and how she had overcome the issue of looking different, and knowing that who she was is on the inside and not on the outside. Karina seemed to take it all in, and little by little, she started to feel more confident.

I also told Karina a story that I had made up. It was about a little frog that worried about the way that he looked. I told her that Flopsie, the frog, was out on a walk one day when a car rode over his foot. His foot was flattened! Flopsie was so embarrassed by his flattened foot that he crawled into a hole and hid from everyone. He did not want anyone to see his flattened foot because he thought that his friends would make fun of him.

The next day, his friends went out looking for him, and could not find him anywhere. They started to call him. "Flopsie, where are you? We miss you! Come out so that we can play!" They walked a little bit farther and called again, "Flopsie, we love you and miss you. We are praying for you, and we miss playing with you. Where are you, Flopsie?"

Finally, Flopsie came out of his hole. He was so happy that his friends still liked him and that they didn't care that his foot looked different. They were thrilled that he was OK.

That was the end of my story.

Karina again seemed to take it all in. After getting the letters and hearing the stories, she went to church, and played with her friends more willingly.

45

"I THINK IT'S TIME FOR you to go back to Lurie Children's Hospital and have an ultrasound on that lump," when the surgeon told us this at her six-month post-op appointment it wasn't easy to hear.

Shortly after surgery in April, I had noticed a lump under the left side of Karina's chin. We were told that it was an enlarged lymph node, but it didn't seem to change with time. It felt like a lima bean was under her skin. It concerned me because it was around the area where her pre-birth tumor had originated. I brought it to the surgeon's attention at each appointment, and he told us in September that if it was the same in October, he would have us get it checked out further.

He first told us to head back to the ENT at Lurie Children's, and I asked him if it would be better to go to the oncology doctors in case it was some kind of tumor. He agreed. So shortly after that, I proceeded to make an appointment with oncology at Lurie Children's Hospital to find out what they thought.

Everything else was going great in regard to Karina's healing. In July, she was able to start moving her left cheek. She noticed the first movement when she was staying overnight at her sister and brother-in-law's house. We were very excited to show her surgeon and all her friends. The more she moved it, the stronger it got. By September, her face moved even when she chewed her food. She practiced smiling in the mirror, and the smile line on the left side of her face was showing more and more.

The orthodontist was also helping Karina again. A tiny molar had come up in the lower left jaw area. It was so wonderful to see, as we didn't know what would come up or when we would ever see it. The two teeth next to it were missing, so this molar would be helpful as an anchor for false teeth, when needed. The orthodontist put expanders in Karina's upper and lower jaws to widen her mouth. She also received rubber bands to pull her teeth in the direction that they needed to go. She was such a good sport, but she had trouble remembering everything that needed to be done daily.

At that point in her life, she was supposed to be wearing her glasses all day and a patch over her right eye for three hours a day (to help with the vision in her left eye). She was also encouraged to be wearing her hearing aid each day. The directions from the orthodontist were to be brushing and using the Waterpik two to three times a day. She was required to wear new rubber bands when she was not eating. She was also supposed to be practicing her smile while looking into a mirror. With the lump under her chin, we were also trying to remember to put some essential oils on it daily.

On the home front, the house we lived in had two acres of land zoned for agriculture. We owned a variety of animals while living there. At that time, we had goats, rabbits, a miniature horse, chickens, dogs, cats, and parakeets. The children received many of their biology lessons while taking care of the animals. They also learned responsibility, care for others, nutrition, birthing processes, and first aid for a variety of breeds of animals.

46

"I'M SORRY, BUT OUR HOSPITAL is out of network for your insurance," the receptionist from Lurie Children's Hospital told me. I had not thought about the fact that in the past eight years, many things had changed. One major change was that Bill had a different job with different insurance. I had decided to make the appointment with the oncologist at Lurie Children's Hospital anyway, but then after talking to some other medical professionals, I realized that it could cost us over $1,000 just for that one check-up appointment.

We reluctantly decided to go a different route. We made an appointment at her pediatrician's office, and from there, he sent her to a hospital in town to have a CT scan of her neck. After getting the results from the scan, we were told that they wanted a new scan, which included Karina's chest. Fast-forward then another week. She had another scan, and we made an appointment at Loyola University Hospital in Chicago to meet with the pediatric oncologists.

It was so hard to start over with new physicians, but going to an in-network hospital was important. This oncologist asked us what had brought us to oncology. I asked her, "Do you want the long story or the short story?" I went with the long story so that she could get a better sense of Karina's past tumor history and her chemo and surgery histories as well.

After the appointment, the oncologist advised us to visit their ENT, as the ENT would be the one to do a biopsy, if it was necessary. I made that next appointment, and then in the meantime, we received the call about the two scans. The radiologist said that the lump seemed to be a stubborn, inflamed lymph node but because of Karina's tumor history, he wanted us to still go ahead with the ENT visit and see what they had to say about it.

At the beginning of December, Karina and our entire family were invited to go to a holiday party that was put on by the cranial-facial clinic at UIC in Chicago. Each year, they put on a fabulous party, including lunch, desserts, crafts, a holiday dance show put on by a nearby dance company, face painting, a strolling balloon artist, and presents for everyone under eighteen. That's right. Everyone was included, even the siblings of patients, and the gifts weren't dollar store gifts, either. They were $15-20 gifts, which had been wrapped and labeled with age and gender so that the children usually received something that was age appropriate.

We all had a great time, and it was an event that Karina especially looked forward to each year. It was a party for her. There were so many other children there with facial abnormalities that she felt comfortable and enjoyed bringing her siblings with her.

47

"CAN YOU PLEASE NOT PLAN the biopsy right before December 17? Karina's big brother is getting married, and I don't want to interfere with his big day," I told the scheduler at Loyola Hospital. I knew that we needed to get the biopsy scheduled, but her big brother's wedding was something that I didn't want her to have to miss because of any unforeseen complications that might occur.

December was always so busy anyway, with programs, parties, caroling, and celebrations. We also had a rehearsal dinner to plan and wedding preparations to prepare. Our family was in charge of the desserts for the wedding. I got her biopsy scheduled for a few days before Christmas.

Armin and Amanda's wedding day was cold, snowy, and blustery, but the wedding taking place inside was beautiful and Christ-honoring. Karina sang a song with her sisters during the ceremony. I had been able to get matching dresses for all the youngest girls who weren't part of the wedding party. One more sibling left the flock of Geaschels to start a new family.

The adjustment of losing her big brother, Armin, was not quite as hard on Karina as losing Britta had been. That was mainly because Armin had been so busy with full-time college, work, and a dating relationship. The girls had all gradually gotten used to him being gone more and more, instead of instantly being gone, as Britta had done two and a half years earlier.

Again, we headed into Chicago for another procedure. That time, we took Jena and Tia with us. Having sisters along gave Karina the companionship that Bill and I couldn't as easily give while traveling.

On the way into Chicago, I sent out a Facebook update and asked for prayer for our day.

Excerpt from CarePages

Dec 21, 2016

We have an early trip into Chicago today. Karina has a questionable lump under her chin. We are thankful for clear roads and warmer temperatures. Our main prayer requests are that Karina would do well emotionally and that the results would come back quickly.

In Christ, Christie

Daddy, Jena, and Tia sat in the waiting room while I went with Karina into the biopsy room. Thankfully, the nurses let me stay with her the entire time. They even moved the furniture around so that I could sit by her head and talk to her during the whole procedure. They told her that the first poke would numb the entire area so that the four biopsies wouldn't hurt.

For some reason, they were wrong. Each poke hurt just as much as the previous one. They had to wiggle the needle to get the desired amount of tissue. She was a real trouper, but she cried silently the entire time. I felt so badly because there was nothing I could do to stop the pain, but I was so thankful that I could stay with her.

They also had originally told us that she was to have no food in the morning before the procedure, so as it was getting close to noon, she was very hungry, which didn't help. Thinking back over all her procedures and scans over the years, her empty tummy was usually her biggest complaint, even as a small baby. It made it that much worse when the technician wondered why we were told that she couldn't eat prior to the biopsy. Next time, I will be sure to question their protocols.

Once the procedure was over and we were released, we found Bill and the girls and then decided to look for the cafeteria. We had food in the car, but it was always nice to spend a little time doing something fun before heading home.

As we left the hospital, we walked past a desk. The cheerful receptionists who had been sitting at the desk came over and handed the girls some new stuffed animals. They were thrilled, especially Tia, as she was handed a black kitty.

During the Christmas season, we waited to get the biopsy results. About ten days later, we received the relieving news that the lump really was only a stubborn, inflamed lymph node. Also during Christmastime, the scab near Karina's ear finally fell off. It had taken from April to December to heal. I figured the new muscle had been catching on the skin near her ear, so every time Karina would smile, the cheek near her ear would be pulled down, which had kept the hole from healing properly.

In January 2017, we again met with the surgeon. He had checked on Karina's progress every four to six weeks since the surgery. He told us that in April he wanted to perform another surgery, to tweak and fine-tune the previous one. Since the muscle was moving in an area where it shouldn't be, he wanted to fix that, as well as to take out some of the fat tissue in the left cheek and/or add fat tissue to the right cheek so that everything would be more symmetrical.

As the months progressed, Karina healed well, and once again, she got back into wearing her glasses full-time. She and Jena each bought

Razor RipSticks in the middle of winter, so they practiced in the dining room. Around the table they went, gaining more and more balance each day as they got back on their RipSticks to practice.

As time went on, Karina gained more self-confidence and became more social with family members and friends. She got over some of her fears and learned to trust God more. As when she was little, she once again loved to sing at the top of her voice, but only if she thought no one was listening to her.

48

"GOD IS GOOD!" THE SURGEON said to us with a huge smile as he pulled his surgical mask down and gave us a thumbs-up. Karina had finally had the next plastic reconstruction done. It was September 19, 2017.

She had been scheduled for the surgery in April, but due to some lingering congestion, we had to postpone the surgery. We rescheduled it for June, as the anesthesiologists preferred to wait six weeks or more for the congestion to be completely gone. When June came around, although Karina had been healthy for five and a half weeks, she once again started to come down with some coughing and congestion.

The day before the scheduled surgery, I called to postpone it for the second time. I told the receptionist that I wanted to wait until after summer to reschedule this surgery. There was too much going on during the summer, things that I did not want her to have to miss. Since it was not something that had to be done right away, we were all OK with waiting.

As September came around, we had another visit with the surgeon. We hadn't seen him since February, and he was very glad that we had waited for the surgery. He told us that April would have worked out, but waiting until September was turning out to be better. Karina's face had continued to heal during that time, and her muscle was working even better than it previously had.

The night before the surgery, Karina said her goodbyes to her sisters, and Bill, Karina, and I headed into Chicago. We again stayed with my cousin and her family, who so graciously had a large bedtime snack ready for us when we arrived. Karina played with the children, and then we headed downstairs to give Karina her pre-surgery shower and get all three of us ready for bed.

Karina was not used to sleeping alone, as she shared a room with seven sisters. She even shared a double bed with one of them (sometimes two of them). She was not excited when she found out about sleeping in a room by herself. In order to help her sleep better, we were able to move a small mattress into the room that Bill and I stayed in, so she could be closer to us.

The next morning, we got up around 5:00 a.m. and got ready. We were at the hospital by 5:55 for the 6:00 appointment. They checked us in, and then we headed to pre-op. Again, the nurses were so cheerful, helpful, and reassuring to Karina.

She showed the first signs of becoming fearful after putting on the hospital gown and getting into the hospital bed. At first, she had been having fun texting with her sisters, but while thinking about them, she started to miss them and realized what was coming next. The pre-op nurse put the TV on for Karina. It helped to take away some of the anxiety, but once in a while, the tears of anticipation would start to flow again.

While in the pre-op room, we were able to speak with the anesthesiologist, the OR nurses, and the surgical team. As they came in one group at a time, each told us what their job was and what they would be doing to care for Karina during surgery.

The surgeon told us that he was not exactly sure what he would find after making the incision but that he had plan A, plan B, and plan C for what he might be able to do. He asked us some questions about certain parts of the surgery, if we wanted them done or not. I asked what he would do if Karina were his daughter, and he assured us that he would go through with all of it. He also assured us that they would take good care of her.

Then once again, Bill asked if he could pray for the team. The surgeon was delighted that Bill would pray. As he finished praying for Karina, the surgeon and other staff members who would be involved left to prep for the surgery.

All too soon, it was time for the nurse to give Karina the medicine to get her sleepy. We explained that she didn't like the medicine and that she would rather have other options. Karina told them that she also didn't want to get the IV put in. So that left option number three, the one we hadn't tried yet and the one that I knew I couldn't handle, the mask.

Karina thought it would be better than her other options until they started wheeling her bed away. She looked back at me and reached out her hand. "Mom, aren't you coming with me?" Oh, my heart, what could I do? The nurse quickly came over with a bundled, soft package and told me to put it on. As I fumbled with it and tried to put the scrubs on over my long skirt while wearing shoes and standing up (because I was in a hurry), the nurse told me that I had to sit down, or I was going to need a hospital bed also.

I got suited up quickly and followed the bed down the hall. One nurse looked at me and said, "I didn't know you were coming with us." I told her that I hadn't known either. Once we arrived in the OR, I was able to help get Karina onto the operating table and then hold her hands while they put on the mask. Unfortunately, she fought it. One nurse had to hold her head while two of us held her arms. Once she was asleep, I was sent out of the room. I then found Bill so that we could await the news when surgery was finished.

We first headed to the cafeteria, where we enjoyed a much-needed and appreciated hot breakfast. Although it was only 8:00, we had been through a lot that morning, and our stomachs thought it was almost noon. We had been told that the surgery might only last one to two hours, so we then headed right back to the OR's waiting room and waited for someone to tell us when surgery was completed. We watched some TV: Chip and Joanna were fixing up houses. I looked through some magazines for ideas regarding the great room, which we were adding on to our house. We talked together and to other parents in the waiting room. I made some phone calls and looked at Facebook and Pinterest.

While we were still in the waiting room, we heard over the hospital loudspeakers that there was free pizza in the cafeteria. It sounded good, and we knew that once Karina was out of surgery, we would not be eating in front of her or leaving her for quite a while. We went back to the cafeteria around 11:00 to get our free pizza.

About that time, Bill got a phone call from one of the OR nurses. She said that Karina's surgery was almost over as they had completed the left side, and that they were just finishing up on the right side. Since we knew that we still had some time, we decided to play ping-pong in the hospital play area. Although the ball was thin and deformed and neither of us had played for quite a while, we enjoyed the activity and the diversion. We were just about equally matched. We played our three games. I won the first game, and Bill won the last two. Then our little buzzer sounded, so we quickly headed back to the waiting room to speak to the surgeon.

A few minutes after we got back in the parent waiting room, the OR door opened and our surgeon came out through it. He was walking quickly. As he pulled down his mask, he revealed a large smile, gave us a thumbs-up, and said, "God is good." He told us that he had been able to accomplish more than he had even planned and that things went better than he had expected. Wow! We were so grateful to the Lord for His kindness.

We learned that the muscle that had been put in during the previous surgery had slipped from the place where they had attached it. So they attended to that first.. Next, the surgeon took out some extra fat from that same cheek area and filled a sunken-in area on the lower part of the jawline. Secondly, while he had the whole area by the ear open, he fixed her ear lobe, which had been distorted because of the tumor. Lastly, he eliminated all the previous scars by making one long thin incision line around her ear, which he glued together instead of using stitches. He was delighted with the surgery, and he told us that we would be able to see her soon.

When arriving in the post-op room to see Karina, I could tell immediately that she was not a happy camper. She was hungry and sore, and she kept trying to talk. Over the years, I had come to realize that she had expectations before surgery, and she remembered them as soon as she woke up.

We turned on the TV for her and found some cartoons that fit the criteria of Mommy and Daddy approved and also were appealing to Karina. They were the ones that Karina had remembered seeing at the hospital during the previous year. The nurse was so kind and tried to help her be more comfortable, but unfortunately, she couldn't give Karina what she really wanted: food. An empty tummy was again her main complaint. Karina was hungry. After getting up early, going through all those awful emotions, and then taking a four-hour nap, her tummy wanted nourishment.

We spent about an hour in the post-op recovery, and then Karina was wheeled to her own room. She and I had planned to stay that night, so our bags and belongings were already in the room. It was not long before Karina had to use the bathroom. We called for a nurse to help with the IV, and Karina and I went into the bathroom. Although she felt the need to go, that part of her had not totally awaken yet. It took a while, but she persevered, and she was finally able to go quite a bit. Feeling better, she got back into bed. It was not long before she was given permission to try some juice, and then she got some yogurt. Getting the food into her tummy really helped her to start feeling better.

The surgeon stopped in before he left for the day and told us that it would be up to us if we went home or stayed the night. Shortly after surgery, I had assumed that we would be staying overnight. As the day progressed, I had thought there might be a chance of going home.

About 4:30 p.m., we were given permission to take her by wheelchair to the cafeteria to get some food. Since it was suppertime, as we went through the line, she got to pick out whatever she wanted within her restrictions. She chose cottage cheese, mashed potatoes, a banana, a Sprite, and ice cream. We could either eat in the cafeteria or take it back to her room. There were also picnic tables outside, so that was Karina's choice.

After eating most of her food, she started to back up her wheelchair, and as she did so, she said, "I'm going to burn off some calories!" With that, she wheeled away, going all over that playground, backward, forward, uphill, and back down, all while Bill and I sat, ate, talked, took videos of her with our phones, and of course, kept an eye on her.

After we were finished outside, she then wanted to wheel herself back to her room, where we would await word of what we were to do next. As she wheeled past her nurses, who were sitting at their station, they looked wide-eyed at her and called her a superstar. I said, "I think we are ready to go home," and they simultaneously agreed.

It still took another hour or so to get the paperwork, the meds, and Karina ready to go. But around 6:00 and just hours after surgery, this miracle child was once again headed home. While traveling, she took selfies on my phone and texted her sisters to let them know we were on our way, because they did not plan on us coming until the next day. I think her sisters were the main reason that she wanted to get home. She loved and missed them, and she did not like the thought of being away from them.

After arriving home, we got the recliner in the living room ready for her, as the surgeon told her to sleep elevated for two weeks. Just the same, as it got closer to her bedtime, she made it clear that she did not want to sleep in the living room with Mom, but in the "dorm room" with her seven sisters. I agreed that she could, as long as she was still elevated and we could put pillows between her and Greta, with whom she shared a double bed.

Her other restrictions were no contact or ball sports for six weeks and no swimming or baths for two weeks. These restrictions made me thankful that she had not had the surgery in April, June, or the middle of summer. It was hard enough in the fall to keep her from these things, but during the summer, it would have been nearly impossible, especially since she felt so good.

The left side of her face was swollen for a few days, as the surgeon told us it would be. After about a week, the left cheek turned red. My first thoughts were, *Is this normal? Is this area finally waking up after surgery? Is this infection?* I made a few calls to the nurses at the hospital, and they finally got back to me and told me to take photos and email them. Thankfully, I had already been taking photos for a few days, just in case something like this happened, so I emailed the photos that I had. It was determined that they were not sure if it was infection, so they prescribed an antibiotic right away, just in case.

Over the next few days, I kept taking photos, but it was hard to decipher if it was improving, getting worse, or staying the same. The nurses said that as long as there was no pain or fever and it was not continuing to swell, we could wait until the following week for her checkup to see the surgeon.

By the day before the two-week checkup, the left cheek looked wonderful. There was no redness, and the swelling had come down a lot. The day before that, there had been some reddish drainage. I was not sure if that had been a good thing. Later, I decided that it must have been, because everything looked great on Monday, October 2, 2017.

Toward the end of November, the surgical glue finally started to peel off. Karina had been careful not to scrub at it or pull it. We just let it fall off on its own. We were then able to see the wonderful job that the surgeon had done to repair past scars and her earlobe, while also carefully closing up the new, large incision. What an art it was to be able to do all that with one thin line of glue.

In December, we were once again able to attend the holiday party in Chicago at the cranial-facial abnormalities clinic. We never did receive our formal invitation in the mail, so per Karina's constant reminders, I called to find out if we were supposed to have received one. The receptionist told me that many people had not received them for some reason. She was glad that I had called, and she wrote down the ages of those from our family who would be attending.

Karina was so happy that we could go, as she had been asking for days when her party would be. The day of the party, all ten of us packed up and headed into Chicago. The girls were dressed in their

Christmas dresses. Elaina, our bird-loving teen, was so thrilled to see a man walking around carrying a large parrot on his shoulder and doing demonstrations with it. He even let her hold it for a short time.

Karina loved the whole event: getting her face painted, eating the extra desserts that she did not normally get at home, seeing her surgeon, and of course, opening her gift. As we were leaving the party, some of the staff members were handing out posters about the movie *Wonder*. Since the movie was about a boy with facial deformities, they were promoting it. One of the Chicago news stations filmed parts of the party for their station so that they could also promote the movie and the theme, "Choose Kind."

After we left the party, our family headed to a large mall near Chicago called Woodfield Mall. The children had never been there, and I realized that I had not been there in over twenty years. We wandered through the mall, only purchasing a few Christmas gifts and then finished our time there eating supper at the A & W Restaurant.

Lastly, we finished our Chicago day by attending a live musical, starring some of our friends. The setting of the musical took place in a canteen during World War II. It happened to be Gramps's birthday that day, so he and Grandma Coco met us at the musical to celebrate. It was a wonderful day that we could enjoy together as a family.

49

"THERE IS NOTHING PLANNED AT this point," I told people after the last procedure that Karina had been through in September. It seemed that most of the concerns that Karina, Bill, and I had at that point in time had been taken care of, and the surgeon himself had nothing new to do. With her face more symmetrical and the muscle put in to help with the smile and her mouth opening wider, it was a good place to stop, wait, and see what God would do with her life.

As of this writing, Karina is only ten and a half years old. Even though most biographies or memoirs don't end abruptly at ten-years-old, I felt it was the best time to write about this chapter in her life and share it with others. Yes, we will continue to meet with her team of surgeons. Yes, there may be more surgeries in the future. Yes, there may be other ways that Karina can be helped and more trials to go through, but at this point, there is nothing new in the plans.

We are so thankful for those who have helped her get to this point. She is more confident in who she is and how God has made her. She is ready to start this new phase with no planned or anticipated future surgeries in the back of our minds.

I pray this story will help you with your faith, as it has helped me with mine. We are not the ones in control, but our God is. We can only control the way that we accept the things that happen in our lives. Are we going to complain about everything? Are we going to find things to be thankful for? Are we going to find help for the things for which we need assistance?

Jesus Christ died for us because we are sinful people. Our trials on earth are minimal compared to the trials that He had to go through because of our sins. If we truly love Him, want to serve Him, and accept His free gift of salvation, everything that we go through is for our good. Although it may not seem like it, those tough situations will have the potential to cause us to depend on Christ and not on ourselves. Romans 8:28 says, "All things work together for good to those who love God, to those who are called according to His purpose." (ESV).

Because of Karina's young life being entrusted to our family and our care, I have learned to be more patient, joyful, peaceful, thankful, understanding, faithful, dependent on God, persistent to research various topics to help my family, and bolder when sharing my faith and story with others. Thank you for taking the time to share in our trials and joys. Our prayer is that you would also find faith, joy, and peace in our Lord and Savior, Jesus Christ.

Acknowledgements

I have always enjoyed writing, but I had never aspired to become a published author. My friend, Grace Johnson, always encouraged me to write a book, and when looking back at all of the countless ways that God helped Karina and our entire family through the first years of her life, I decided that her story would be the first one that I would write. I am so thankful for the support of my husband Bill, and all of our children (and their families), our siblings, and our parents who supported me in the writing of this book.

My thanks also goes to Christ's Church, Rock Valley Bible Church, First Free Church, the Cornerstone Class, Jan Van Dellen, Rebecca Burwell, Anna Rossi, Megan Blick, Ashley Bedgood, and Virginia Polizzi… for all of the prayers and the countless ways that many of you helped our family in the beginning of this story, and then others of you helped in the later years of this writing.

I also want to thank the many doctors, nurses, therapists, and others who have had a hand or voice in the caring of our dear Karina Faith. Thank you for investing your time and expertise to help Karina and so many others.

My thanks to:

- Vickie and Jude (midwives)
- Fran and Marla (therapists)
- Center for Sight and Hearing (audiology)
- Children's Memorial Hospital (NICU, oncology, plastics, ENT, and pathology)
- DSCC (who has paid for so many of Karina's doctor bills, glasses, and hearing aids)
- Loyola Hospital (oncology, ENT, pathology)
- Lurie Children's Hospital (plastics)
- Orthodontic Specialties (orthodontic care)
- Prentice Hospital/ Northwestern University (maternal-fetal, NICU)
- Rockford Memorial Hospital (maternal-fetal and vision department)
- Shriners Hospital (micro-plastics)
- 1st Step Chiropractic (chiropractic care)
- Swedish American Hospital (imaging department)
- UIC Craniofacial Clinic in Medical District, Chicago (Craniofacial)
- University of Illinois at Chicago Hospital (plastics and CT)

References

Berg, Carolina Sandell. "Day by Day." *The Worshipping Church Hymnal*, 367 Carol Stream: Hope Publishing Company, 1990.

Rippon, John. "How Firm a Foundation," *The Worshipping Church Hymnal*, 612 Carol Stream: Hope Publishing Company, 1990

04089936-00835833

Printed in the United States
by Baker & Taylor Publisher Services